THE
GREAT
LOBSTER
COOKBOOK

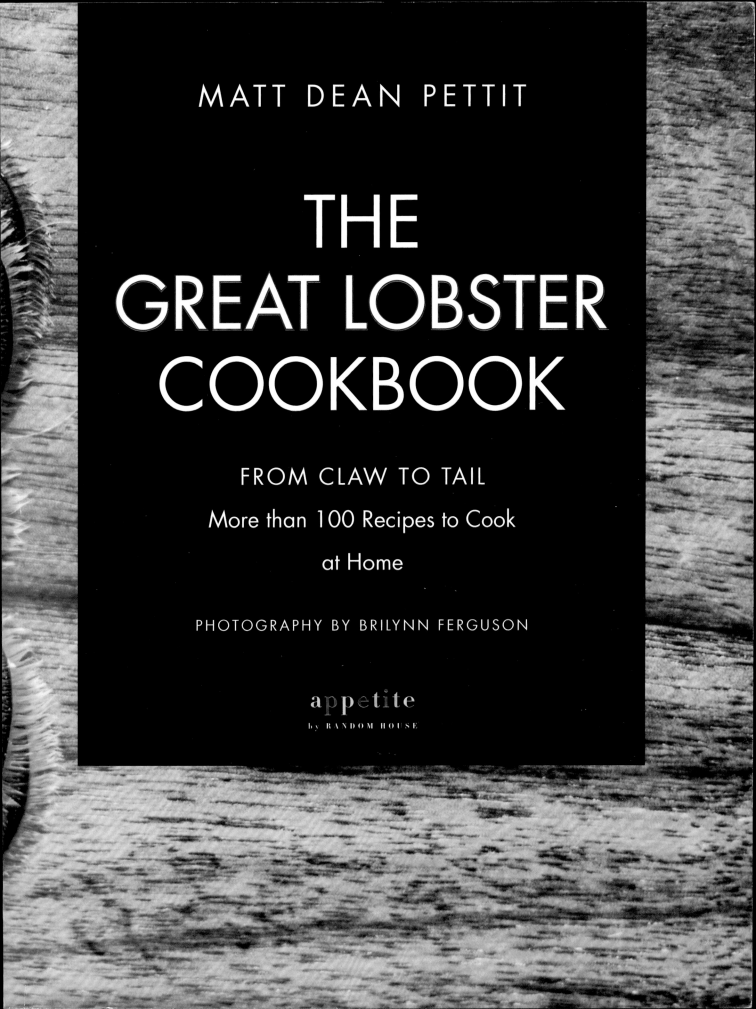

MATT DEAN PETTIT

THE
GREAT LOBSTER
COOKBOOK

FROM CLAW TO TAIL

More than 100 Recipes to Cook

at Home

PHOTOGRAPHY BY BRILYNN FERGUSON

appetite
by RANDOM HOUSE

Appetite by Random House® is a registered trademark of Random House LLC

Library and Archives of Canada Cataloguing in Publication
is available upon request.

Print ISBN: 978-0-449-01628-2
e-book ISBN: 978-0-449-01629-9

Cover and book design by Terri Nimmo
Photography by Brilynn Ferguson
Illustrations on pages 10-11 and 12-13 by Donald Pettit
Nautical flags on pages 197-204 © Jonathan Hurley/Dreamstime.com

Printed and bound in China

Published in Canada by Appetite by Random House®,
a division of Random House of Canada Limited,
a Penguin Random House Company

www.randomhouse.ca

10 9 8 7 6 5 4 3 2 1

They say you can't pick your family
but I wouldn't have it any other way!

Love you, guys.

Thank you for making me
the man I am today. xox

Contents

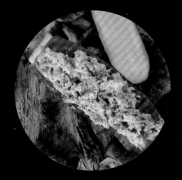

INTRODUCTION

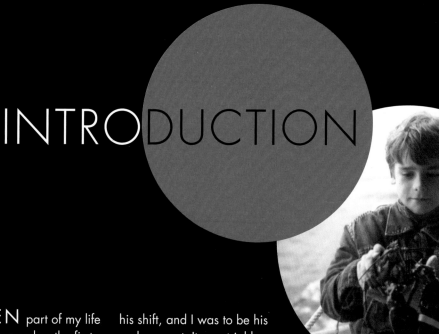

LOBSTER HAS BEEN part of my life since I was a little boy. I can still remember the first time I tasted it, on a family road trip to the east coast of Canada. We had loaded up the car and set out on our journey, from my hometown of Midland, Ontario, to Wolfville, Nova Scotia, to see a family friend. At every pit stop, we visited roadside shacks that served bright red lobsters—and people were eating them with their hands! I could barely believe my eyes. People eating with their hands? When you're nine years old, anything you can eat with your hands is a dream come true! Since that magical moment, I've been hooked, and every year after that for my birthday I would ask, without fail, for a bib, hot butter, and a lobster the size of my body.

When I was 13 years old, I got my first job— working as a busboy at Casey's Restaurant, the hotspot in my hometown at the time. At age 14, I was promoted to kitchen prep, and fell in love with it right away. I continued to work in kitchens through-out high school, cooking and learning about all different types of food, but it was my job at The BoatWorks when I was 16 that stands out the most. The BoatWorks sat right on the water and was the busiest place in town. It was there that I got my first chance to cook and work with seafood. I vividly remember the first day the chef put me on the raw bar. The regular oyster shucker hadn't shown up for

his shift, and I was to be his replacement. It was trial by fire, and I was forced to learn how to shuck 800 oysters on the spot . . . I still have all my fingers today, so I think we can say the shift was a success!

For the next few years, I worked in the kitchens of many great restaurants, learning from many amazing people, all stoking the fire in my belly to one day start my own place. I was always told that "you have two ears and one mouth for a reason." I took that lesson to heart, and I would listen carefully and learn about all things seafood and lobster whenever possible. When I was in university, my lucky roommates would often be treated to a home-cooked Sunday meal (Grizzy and Spano, you remember, right?). We could always find a spot in our nonexistent student budget for some lobster tails, some crab legs, and a 12-pack of beer. I was never intimated by the prospect of cooking lobster. I just loved experimenting with it, and if I was lucky enough to spot one on a restaurant menu, it was a given that I would order it.

Many years later, in 2011, I was working in a suit-and-tie day job in Toronto when I had a life-changing lobster experience. My girlfriend, Dana, and I had been invited to our friends Darcy and Jen's wedding in Miramichi, New Brunswick. While there, we had the good fortune to experience Maritime hospitality at its finest. Maritimers are wonderful, hard-working people who would give you the shirt off their back if you needed it—if you have ever been out east, I'm sure you know what I mean. Many of them make their living from the sea, and lobsters and seafood are just everywhere! It was as if the lobsters were inviting me to eat them from every storefront, and I happily accepted their invitation! In New Brunswick, lobsters are available everywhere—in dive bars and restaurants, and straight from the dock. You can even buy live lobsters at the airport and have them packed while you wait for your flight! And it was while I was sitting in the airport waiting for my flight that I started to think more about lobster. I got to thinking about the perceptions that people have about lobster and wondering why this delicious crustacean that I love so much isn't more readily available to everyone. . . . And suddenly a lightbulb went on inside my head.

I decided right there and then that I would bring lobster to the people! No matter how far from the ocean they lived. From that point on I made it my mission to:

1) Make lobster more accessible for everyone

2) Challenge the way we cook lobster and create new ways to prepare and serve it

3) Take any pretentiousness away from lobster.

Rock Lobster Food Co.

When I got back from New Brunswick, I knew I had to put my mission into action. But where to start? I had previously heard of a cool new concept called the Toronto Underground Market (TUM), a food market for budding chefs and food-entrepreneurs, and in September 2011, I decided to pay it a visit. Entrepreneurial food markets are not anything new, but this one stood out from the crowd: excellent vendors, perfect venue, amazing musical acts, and a great list of local libations (craft beers and premium tequila). TUM then tossed

in 2,000 food lovers and had itself a serious jam! As I walked through the venue, I was in awe of the great passion and energy radiating from every vendor. It absolutely blew me away, and I knew I had to be a part of it.

I went home immediately and started what felt like a "Jerry Maguire" 14-hour writing binge. One week and 30 pages of chicken scratch later, the idea for Rock Lobster Food Co. was born. This pseudo-business plan/hybrid mission statement outlined every single detail, from the name of the company ("rock" as in rock 'n' roll and "lobster," of course, as the star of the menu—thank you, DC, for your help on that one) to the brand colors, staff uniforms, marketing plan, logo, and menu.

Popping-up

On March 8, 2012, I launched the first ever Rock Lobster pop-up event. Some of my friends worked at a prominent hotel in downtown Toronto and kindly let me host the launch there. Preparing for it was, to be completely honest, the scariest thing I have ever done. I took roughly $2,500 of my savings and bought some starter cooking equipment, then created basic signage and cool staff shirts, and built a table (with employee #2, my boy Matty C) in the basement of my condo parking lot. This amount of money may not seem like a large investment for many, but I tell you, it was for me.

When the day of the event was upon us, I rallied employee #1, Dana, and a few close friends to help set up the location. I had seen the social media interest that other companies had generated using Twitter and Facebook, so I started a little social media effort of my own, promoting the event in hopes of attracting some customers. The doors opened at 5 p.m., and by 6 p.m. there was a line down the street. Between all the social media foodies and people who just happened to be passing by, we sold 350 lobster rolls in a few short hours. It was crazy! It was the beginning! Rock Lobster Food Co. had officially arrived.

The Rock Lobster concept quickly took off. Many more pop-up events followed, as well as my first TUM vendor experience—I remember fist-pumping the air when I got the email accepting us for the April 2012 event! In the early days, we would prep for an event until 6 a.m., and most times be up and ready to go at the event site only a few hours later. I learned quickly that the art of the pop-up was being able to travel to showcase and sell your food and concept to as many food lovers as possible. We quickly gained a strong media following, which got more people behind the idea of making lobster and seafood more readily available to Canadians. My small team and I developed a very strong fan base, and as our fan base and media following grew, so did our opportunities. In early September 2012, I was lucky enough to be introduced to my current business partners— Darryl Fine and Alan Thomson, who have 60 plus years of restaurant and bar experience between them—and joined forces with them to take Rock Lobster to the next level.

The Restaurants

On December 1, 2012, we opened our first Rock Lobster Food Co. restaurant in the heart of Ossington village in Toronto. Ossington was the perfect place for us to take Rock Lobster to the next level—and our neighbors welcomed us with open arms. You will even see a recipe in this book by Rocco, the chef and co-owner of Pizza Libretto, who added a "welcome to the neighborhood" Rock Lobster Pizza special to his menu for us one night! And, even better, they sold out early in the evening. I truly appreciated his gesture—it was a real sign of great friendship and good things to come.

On July 16, 2013, after just seven months of packing the house nightly in Ossington, we opened our second Rock Lobster location. You might think I'm crazy (and sometimes I'd agree), but we were turning away more guests than we could have possibly imagined, and a second location meant more lobster for more people! At our second location on Queen Street West in Toronto, we have been able to add an amazing back patio that

instantly makes you feel like you're at a cottage in Nova Scotia or Maine. I have also been able to create an in-house fresh seafood market, where guests can walk in off the street and purchase many different kinds of fresh seafood daily. Or, after a meal, our guests can order the same products they just enjoyed in the restaurant to take home with them. I'm still amazed that people can take home our Matty's Seafood product line, which includes fresh and frozen seafood, bisques, chowders, and more, to enjoy with their friends and family.

The Next Chapter

What an incredible ride it's been: I've gone from scribbling an idea on paper to having a small pop-up/catering company with a three-foot food stall to being the proud chef and owner of two award-winning Rock Lobster restaurants, hosting countless sell-out events, and even cooking for the Queen of Cooking herself, Martha Stewart! We have been nominated for Best New Restaurant, won Best Caesar (Canada's national cocktail), been named one of the Top 5 Restaurants in Toronto, and, of course, won Best Lobster Roll in Toronto. Our company has gone from 1 employee to over 80 in just a few years! I am having the time of my life, because I had a goal, followed my mission, and always work with the best people around. I would like to dedicate this book to my family, friends, our loyal fans, and anyone who has taken a leap of faith to follow their heart, passion, and dreams.

So, what's next for Rock Lobster Food Co.? Well, no rest for the wicked, that's for sure. If you remember, my initial goal was to bring lobster to the masses, and I won't stop until I've done that. This cookbook brings me one giant step closer to my goal.

Join the Crustacean Nation!

Cheers!

Matt Dean Pettit

LOBSTER 101

HOW TO USE THIS BOOK

In this cookbook, I'm going to teach you all about lobster, including how to buy lobster, properly cook lobster, and eat lobster. And, most important, I'll share my lobster recipes, which range from super-easy and fun for parties to perfect dishes for your next black tie affair. I promise that this book will give you the same passion for lobster that I have and will teach you all you need to know about preparing lobster at home.

PREPPING AND INGREDIENTS

There are a huge variety of dishes you can make with lobster, but there are really only a few straightforward ways to cook it for using it in those dishes. Once you've mastered the handful of cooking methods (boiling, parboiling, steaming, and grilling), the world's your oyster. I've included directions for all of these, for both live and frozen lobsters (including cooking time cheat sheets), on pages 17–19.

For the recipes in this book, there are lots of ingredients that crop up again and again and that are basically prepped or bought the same way each time. To make your life easier, here's a list of things that you can take as standard in this book (any exceptions are noted in the recipe):

- Shrimp is uncooked
- Eggs are large
- Fruit and vegetables are medium, skin on, and are washed before using
- Bell and jalapeño peppers have their seeds removed
- Tomatoes have their seeds removed
- Onions are yellow
- Green onions are used whole (white and green parts)
- Lemon, lime, and orange juices are all freshly squeezed
- Spinach has its stems removed
- Herbs have their stems removed
- Pepper is black
- Salt is table salt
- Milk is 2%

- Mayonnaise and sour cream are full fat
- Butter is at room temperature (but salted or unsalted is specified in the recipe)
- Cream cheese is plain and at room temperature
- Flour is all-purpose
- Olive oil is any grade
- Maple syrup is any grade (but not pancake syrup)

ICONS

I've included some icons for the recipes so that you learn a bit more about them just by glancing at the page:

 Classics are just that, classic. These are recipes for the dishes that sell like crazy in the Rock Lobster restaurants, like my Rock Lobster Roll (page 101).

 This icon highlights dishes that are great for sharing. In the restaurants, we usually suggest sharing two of these dishes per person.

 I am very honored to have good friends in the restaurant trade, who also happen to be culinary masters! This icon represents a recipe that has been written by one of five world-class chefs: Mark McEwan, Claudio Aprile, Roger Mooking, Rob Gentile, and Rocco Agostino. These guys didn't miss a beat when I asked them to contribute their favorite lobster recipe to this book, and you'll find them on pages 52, 88, 128, 138 and 146.

THE LOBSTER

Are you sitting comfortably? Your lob-ducation—all you need to know about our favorite crustacean—is about to begin.

A lobster's size is assessed by its weight in pounds.

LOBSTER SPECIES

Experts believe there are around 48 known lobster species around the world. The best-known three are described below.

American lobster (*Homarus americanus*)

This species of lobster is found on the US and Canadian Atlantic coast, from Labrador all the way down to southern New Jersey. American lobsters are usually greenish brown in color and have red spines. Having said that said, over the years fisherman have caught bright neon blue, orange, and even albino lobsters. These colors are due to rare pigment mutations, and the odds of catching a lobster in one of these colors is 1 in 100 million! American lobsters usually weigh between 1.25 lb and 1.5 lb each, although they can go up to over 5 lb. In 1977, a lucky fisherman pulled in one weighing 44.4 lb off the coast of Nova Scotia! This remains a Guinness World Record for the largest American lobster ever caught. For a full anatomy breakdown on American lobsters, turn to page 12.

European lobster (*Homarus gammarus*)

The European lobster is cousin to our American lobster, but smaller (lobster legend has it that the largest one caught weighed 13 lb). They look somewhat similar (both have two front claws), but the European's claws are smaller, and European lobsters are generally blue. They're found mainly across the northeastern Atlantic Ocean from northern Norway to Morocco, but are most commonly found along the coasts of the UK, Ireland, and France. These lobsters feed on mollusks, crabs, and, rumor has it, their fellow European lobsters.

Forty years ago, criminals would riot because they were sick and tired of eating this now coveted ingredient.

Spiny/Caribbean/Rock lobster (*Palinuridae*)

The third most-famous and commercially important lobster in the world is known by three different names. Unlike the American and European lobsters, spiny lobsters live and thrive in warm waters in places like Mexico, Australia, New Zealand, and

Caribbean countries. They are not closely related to the American or European lobster at all—for starters, they are *much* bigger, and they're all tail (I've seen them in Mexico and Cuba with tails as long as a child's arm!). They also have very, very small claws, and use huge, thick antennae for protection instead. Their meat is less sweet and tender than that of our other two lobster species.

Lobsters can grow up to three feet long, and have teeth in their stomach, head, and kidneys.

For this book, I created the recipes using American lobster, because, in my humble opinion, it's the best-tasting lobster in the world! But it's also the lobster that's local for me and my restaurants, and eating locally sourced lobster gets my vote every time. If you use European or spiny lobster for any of the recipes in the book, just be mindful of the size difference and modify the quantities accordingly.

Lobsters grow back limbs—claws or antennae, for example—that they lose in battle. It is only if they lose their tail that they can't survive.

LOBSTER FISHING

Commercial lobster fishing really took off in the mid-1800s with the invention of the enclosed stamp can (the cans we use these days for tuna or soup). Stamp cans meant that normally perishable seafood could start to be safely transported. In those days, fishermen would spear the lobsters. They would set out to catch (spear!) as many as they could, regardless of size, because they would sell them by the piece rather than by the pound like they do today. Today, the most common method of lobster fishing in Canada and America is by lobster trap (or pot). Traps are set by lines, with multiple traps per line, and are dropped onto the seafloor. The fishing seasons vary across Canada and the USA. As one

Lobsters navigate by smell. They also taste with their feet and hear with their legs.

area closes, another opens. Fishermen head out very early—way before sunrise—in hopes of pulling in full lobster pots. They bring their catch to the dock, where seafood buyers (processing companies) are waiting to buy the tasty crustaceans. The lobsters are sold per pound, and the price fluctuates frequently, accordingly to the time of year and the basic principles of supply and demand. The processors then take the lobsters to their lobster pounds and sell them on to restaurants and retailers.

Lobster fishing is more than a job; it's a way of life. To make a living from it is a daily battle. If you ask me, it has to be one of the hardest jobs on the planet. I've got to know some amazing fishermen personally, through my trips to Nova Scotia, and I have to tip my hat to them for the tough daily grind they go through.

Originally, lobsters served two purposes: to feed prisoners and servants, and to be used as fertilizer.

The next time you're having fun preparing and eating lobster, take a moment to appreciate the efforts of the hard-working, dedicated people who were behind that lobster making its way to your plate.

Sustainability

The number of lobsters in the ocean waters around Canada and the USA is at an all-time high. One factor that has led to this abundance is global warming: as waters are becoming warmer, lobsters are being born more frequently and growing faster and larger. Another major contributing factor has

Lobsters do not feel pain. They have a decentralized nervous system. The sound that you hear when you put them in

boiling water is actually the sound of gases being released from their shells, and not squealing.

been the lobster sustainability movement. Lobster sustainability means government fishery boards monitor lobster fishing very closely, and put measures in place to protect the number—and size—of lobsters that can be taken from the ocean. The goal is to ensure that lobster fishing is carried out in a way that protects and conserves the lobster population, and promotes its growth and reproduction. Lobster sustainability is crucial to making sure that lobsters remain in our oceans for many years to come.

It is near impossible to determine the age of a lobster, so it's estimated by their weight: it takes about 6 years for a lobster to grow to 1 lb.

Sustainability is a global issue. Cuba, for example, depends on lobster as it's one of its top exports. In Canada and the USA, lobster fishing is the most financially valuable sector of the fishing industry. So, lobster sustainability will protect not only our beloved lobsters but also our economies. Some of the rules governing lobster fishing in Canada include fishermen only being allowed to fish during specific times of the year, and limits being placed on both the number of fishing permits issued, and the number of lobsters that can be caught by each fisherman. Lobster traps must be a specific size, and it is illegal to keep a berried (pregnant) female lobster or a lobster smaller than 1 lb.

LOBSTER LINGO

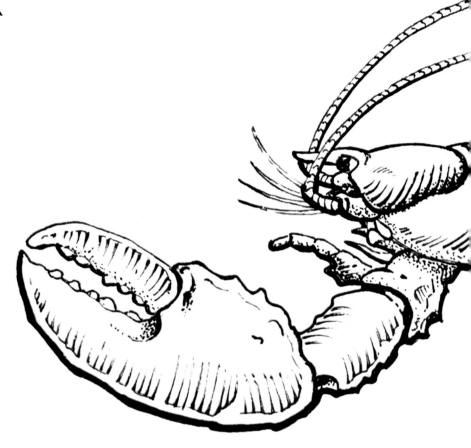

BERRIED FEMALE
Female lobster carrying fertilized eggs in its tail flippers (swim-merets).

● ● ●

CANNER
Small lobster, weighing ½–1 lb.

CHICKEN
Lobster weighing around 1 lb.

COCK
Male lobster.

CORAL
Roe or eggs that the female hasn't released to her tail yet. It's safe to eat and is considered a delicacy. Think of it as lobster caviar.

CRUSHER CLAW
The larger of the lobster's two claws. It can be on the right or the left side, meaning that a lobster can be left- or right-handed.

CULL
Lobster that has lost one or both claws (don't worry, these can grow back naturally as the lobster molts and grows).

CUTTER
The smaller of the lobster's two claws. It cuts prey and holds it in place. It's also known as the pincher claw.

● ● ●

EIGHTH
Lobster weighing 1 ⅛ lb.

● ● ●

HARD-SHELL
Lobster whose new shell has completely hardened.
It has 50%–60% more meat than a soft-shell lobster and is more nutritious than a soft-shell lobster.

HEN
Female lobster.

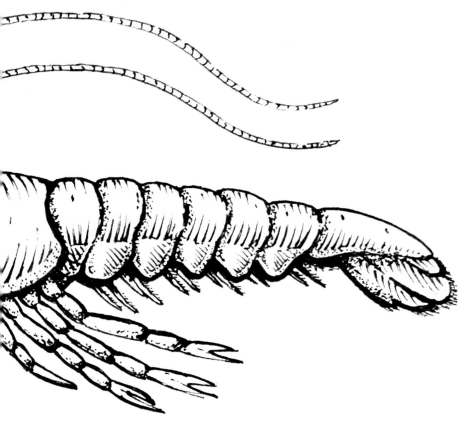

• • •

QUARTER
Lobster weighing 1 ¼ lb.

• • •

SHORT
Lobster that is legally too small to keep and must be thrown back into the ocean.

SOFT-SHELL LOBSTER (ALSO KNOWN AS A SHEDDER)
Lobster that has recently molted (see above). It has very little flesh and a very soft texture, and the taste is not as sweet as that of a hard-shell lobster. Soft-shell lobsters do not travel well, and are often shipped frozen or precooked. They're less expensive than hard-shell lobsters.

• • •

TOMALLEY
This green creamy foam material is the lobster's liver and pancreas. Like coral, it's considered a delicacy.

• • •

V-NOTCH
Lobster fishermen must make a notch in the middle flipper piece of the tail of any berried female lobster that they catch before they toss it back into the ocean. Catching berried lobsters is illegal, and the notch helps other fishermen identify the lobsters at a glance.

• • •

JUMBO
Lobster weighing over 2 ½ lb.

• • •

LARGE
Lobster weighing 1 ½–2 ½ lb.

LFA
Lobster fishing area.

• • •

MOLTING
The process by which lobsters grow. Lobsters shed their shells roughly once a year (like a snake sheds its skin) and grow them back larger each time. During the growing-back process, the off-season, lobsters are known as "soft-shell" (see right).

• • •

PISTOL
Lobster that has lost both its claws (don't worry, they grow back!).

LOBSTER

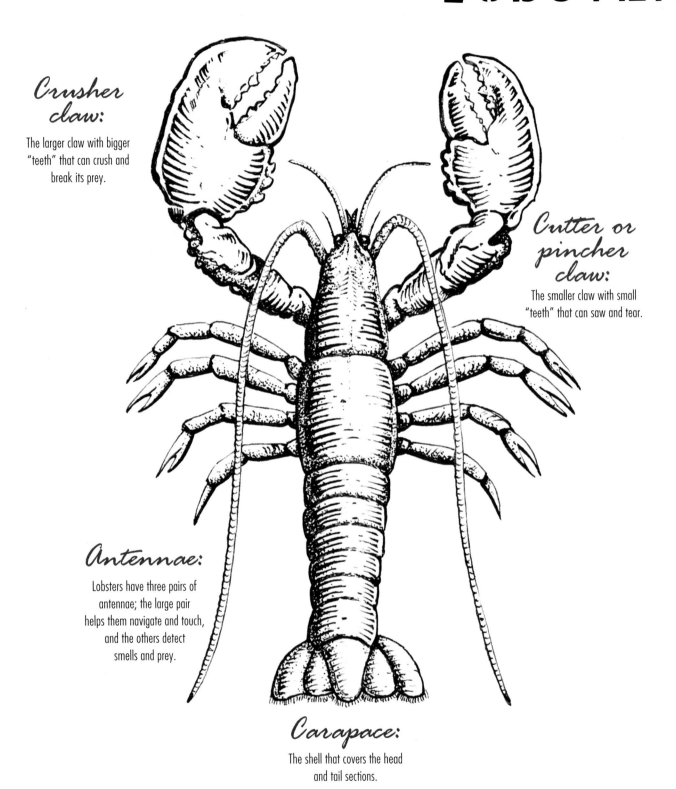

Crusher claw:

The larger claw with bigger "teeth" that can crush and break its prey.

Cutter or pincher claw:

The smaller claw with small "teeth" that can saw and tear.

Antennae:

Lobsters have three pairs of antennae; the large pair helps them navigate and touch, and the others detect smells and prey.

Carapace:

The shell that covers the head and tail sections.

ANATOMY

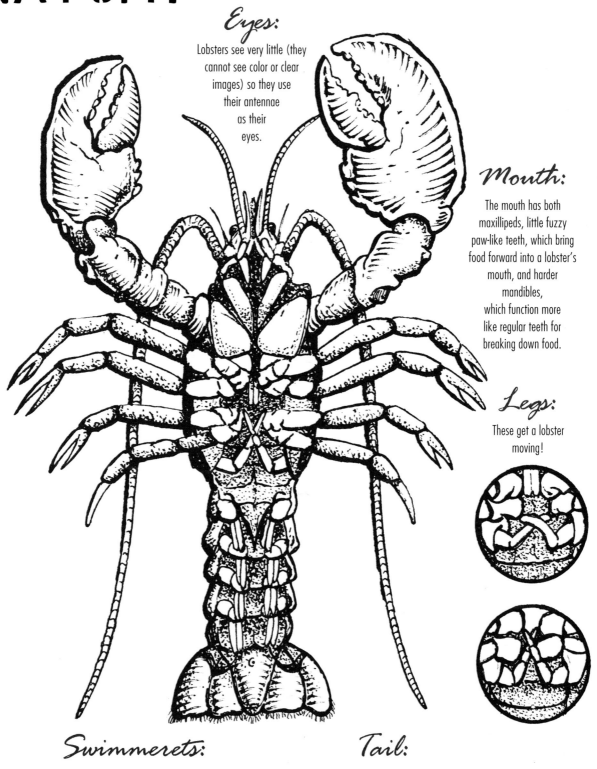

Eyes:

Lobsters see very little (they cannot see color or clear images) so they use their antennae as their eyes.

Mouth:

The mouth has both maxillipeds, little fuzzy paw-like teeth, which bring food forward into a lobster's mouth, and harder mandibles, which function more like regular teeth for breaking down food.

Legs:

These get a lobster moving!

Swimmerets:

Five small pairs of fins underneath the tail that help a lobster navigate when swimming. These are also used to determine sex, as female lobsters carry their eggs in them.

Tail:

Six segments called uropods with the telson holding them together located in the middle at the end of the tail. This looks like a fan of feathers.

HOW TO BUY AND STORE LOBSTER

LIVE LOBSTERS
Buying from a Store

If you're planning to purchase live lobsters from a store, there are a few simple rules to follow:

- Choose a store that sells a lot of lobsters, like a fish market, so you can be confident that it is as fresh as possible.
- Look at the lobster tank. The tank should be clean, the water should be clear, and the lobsters should not be packed in tightly like, well, sardines.
- Pick a lobster that is lively and moving around, and that moves vigorously when held. Ideally, you should choose one with its tail sticking out straight and not curled (this is a sign of fatigue and the lobster could be near death).

Buying from the Source

There are a lot of great suppliers out there whom you can contact directly and who will even ship live lobster to your door. For the best prices year-round, simply find out which fishing area is in season and order your live lobsters directly from there!

Storing

You must store live lobsters properly. As soon as a lobster dies, its meat starts to decompose and is no longer safe to eat. As soon as you get home with your lobsters, put them in a paper bag, cover them with a wet newspaper or wet paper towel, and store them on the bottom shelf of the refrigerator. Remember: a dry lobster is an angry lobster, so wet that newspaper regularly to keep it damp! Never store the lobsters on ice or tap water as both will quickly kill them. Lobsters stored properly should stay alive for 24–48 hours.

FROZEN LOBSTERS
Buying Frozen Lobster Meat

The technology for freezing meat has drastically improved in the last decade, so much so that many restaurants across the world now buy frozen lobster. The seafood processor will quickly steam-cook live lobsters, then remove the meat and vacuum-seal it in brine. Many processors are now specializing in premium frozen meat, where they package the best parts (the tail, knuckle, and claw meat) in vacuum bags. If you're in a pinch (excuse the pun), you can buy canned frozen lobster meat, but I wouldn't recommend it—it always seems to have a metallic taste.

Buying Frozen Lobster Tails

You can buy two types of lobster tails:

- American lobster tails (cold water tails) are the most common lobster tail in grocery stores and restaurants in Canada and America. This meat will be whiter, more tender, and sweeter—and therefore more expensive—than the meat of warm water lobster tails.

• Spiny/Caribbean/rock lobster tails (warm water tails) are also available in most grocery stores and are usually significantly cheaper than American tails. It's common to see these frozen tails with a lot of glazing (the result of suppliers injecting water between the shell and the tail to protect the tail during shipping and storage, which leaves them looking buffered, almost as if they are covered in ice). This increases the weight, which increases the cost, as you pay by weight.

If I had to choose one, I would choose the American lobster tail, and I believe that most chefs would agree that cold water lobsters have far superior meat. Never buy frozen lobster tails with a lot of glazing, or that look yellow or gray. Always keep it as fresh as possible!

Storing
Store frozen lobster meat and tails in the freezer, in an airtight bag or container, for up to 3 months.

PREVIOUSLY COOKED
Try to avoid buying a previously cooked whole lobster as they are never the best quality. If you do, though, be sure to follow these rules:

• Ensure the lobster has bright, shiny eyes.
• Do not buy the lobster if you smell a strong odor—it should have a nice aroma.
• Make sure that the lobster has a curled tail as this indicates that it was alive when it was cooked.

Storing
Store previously cooked lobster meat in the fridge, in an airtight bag or container, for up to 3 days.

HOW TO COOK LOBSTER

It's time to start cooking lobster! Whether you picked out a great fresh live lobster, or you have frozen lobster tails ready to go, it's showtime! Don't be scared. It's a widespread misconception that lobster is hard to cook, but you shouldn't be intimidated, it really is very straightforward.

A lobster is cooked when it turns bright red. Another good test is to pull at one of the legs. If it comes off easily, you know it's done. If cooked properly, the meat will be sweet and tender—it's easy to overcook a lobster, which makes the meat very dry, so always keep a careful eye on cooking times.

COOKING LIVE LOBSTER

You can cook a live lobster by boiling, parboiling, steaming, or grilling it. Select which method is best for the dish you are preparing. If the recipe indicates a particular method, that's what you should do. You must cook lobster alive or kill it immediately before cooking. Don't worry, lobsters don't feel pain. If you don't like to handle the lobster while it is moving, stick it in the freezer for around 20 minutes prior to cooking, or lay it on its back for a couple of minutes. Both of these things will put it in a catatonic state.

COURT BOUILLON

Court bouillon is a French term (its literal translation is "short broth"). It's a fancy-sounding term for a light stock used in dishes where the main ingredients are only cooked in the stock for a short time. You can prepare the stock in advance and refrigerate it in an airtight container for up to 4 days or freeze for up to 2 months. Just be sure to allow it to cool before placing in the refrigerator or freezer.

8 quarts water
1 tsp kosher salt
2 large white onions, roughly chopped
1 head celery, roughly chopped
1 bulb fennel, roughly chopped
4 orange skins
2 lemons, halved
10 black peppercorns
4 bay leaves

1. Fill a large stockpot with the water and add the kosher salt. Add the onions, celery, and fennel, along with the orange skins, lemon halves, peppercorns, and bay leaves. Bring the liquid to a boil over high heat, then turn down the heat to medium. Cover and simmer for 15 to 20 minutes, allowing the flavors to infuse.

Makes 8 quarts (enough to boil 2 lobsters)

Boiling

Boiling is one of the simplest ways to cook lobster. Follow the method below for perfect boiled lobster (the directions I give here are good for cooking two lobsters at a time). My classic Court Bouillon recipe (see sidebar on page 17) is a must, as it will add a lot of flavor.

1. In a large stockpot, prepare the Court Bouillon (page 17) and bring it to a boil.
2. Prepare an ice bath in a bucket or the sink. You'll need it for submerging the lobster immediately after boiling to stop it from overcooking.
3. Remove the plastic bands from the lobsters' claws just before you put them in the pot.
4. Using tongs, submerge the lobsters in the broth. Cover and boil over high heat, using the cheat sheet to guide you on timings. The lobsters will turn bright red when cooked.
5. Using tongs, remove each steamed lobster from the pot and hold them upside down to let any excess stock drain out.
6. Place the lobsters in the ice bath for a couple of minutes to cool.

> ### CHEAT SHEET
>
> ## LOBSTER BOILING
>
> | Lobster Size | Cooking Time |
> |---|---|
> | 1 lb | 7 minutes |
> | 1 ⅛ lb | 9 minutes |
> | 1 ¼ lb | 10 minutes |
> | 1 ½–2 lb | 12 minutes |
> | 2 lb | 13–14 minutes |
> | 3 lb | 16 minutes |
>
> TIP: If boiling soft-shell rather than hard-shells lobsters, cut the cooking time by 2 minutes per pound.

Poaching and Parboiling

Use this simple technique when you only need to cook the lobster halfway through before adding it to a recipe. This will prevent the lobster from being overcooked and dried out.

1. Follow the directions for boiling lobster, but reduce the cooking time to 3 to 4 minutes per pound. If in doubt, undercook a little rather than risk overcooking.
2. Drain the lobster and place in an ice bath, as you would if boiling.

Steaming

Some people swear by boiling lobster, others say that only steaming will do. I think both methods have their advantages. Steaming lobsters is certainly safer because you're not dealing with a big pot of boiling liquid, and if you steam the lobster correctly, it will have a great flavor and tender texture. Here is a fail-safe way to steam lobster perfectly every time.

1. Prepare an ice bath in a bucket or the sink. You'll need it for submerging the lobster immediately after steaming to stop it from overcooking.
2. Add 2 inches of water and lots of kosher salt to a large pot. Be liberal with the salt—the water should taste like seawater.
3. Place a steaming rack in the pot and bring the water to a rolling boil over high heat.

CHEAT SHEET

LOBSTER STEAMING

Lobster Size	Cooking Time
1 lb	8 minutes
1 1/8 lb	10 minutes
1 1/4 lb	12 minutes
1 1/2–2 lb	14 minutes
2 lb	16–17 minutes
3 lb	20 minutes

TIP: If steaming soft-shell rather than hard-shells lobsters, cut the cooking time by 2 minutes per pound.

4. Remove the plastic bands from the lobsters' claws just before you put them in the pot.
5. Place the live lobsters, head first, into the pot and cover quickly with a lid to trap the steam. Cook over high heat, using the cheat sheet to guide you on timings. The lobsters will turn bright red when cooked.
6. Using tongs, remove the steamed lobsters from the pot and hold them upside down to let any excess water drain out.
7. Place the lobsters in the ice bath for a couple of minutes to cool.

Grilling

The summer has arrived, you have a drink in your hand, and the barbecue is on—life is good! I grew up in a small town that had a very strong summer cottage community. It was great growing up around the barbecue, and I now consider myself a grill master (self-proclaimed, of course). I prefer charcoal over gas, but either way, grilling adds a rich, smoky flavor to lobster meat. It also allows you to enjoy the great outdoors.

1. Before you cook the lobster, stick it in the freezer for 20 minutes to make it docile. When you take it out of the freezer, insert a large, sharp knife into the center of its head to kill it instantly. Split the live lobster in half lengthwise through the entire body. Be very careful as you slice. Remove the tomalley (liver) or any roe (coral) and wash the body under cold running water for 10 seconds.
2. Prepare the marinade (see sidebar). Then head out to the grill.
3. Ensure the grill is clean. Using paper towel, wipe it with vegetable or canola oil to prevent the meat from sticking once it's hot. If you are cooking with charcoal, ensure that the coals are extremely hot. If you are cooking on a gas grill, set it to medium-high heat, 350°F–375°F.
4. Place the lobster halves, shell side down, on a cutting board. Crack both claws just enough to break their shell.
5. Season the halves with kosher salt and freshly ground black pepper and drizzle the cracked claws with half of the marinade.
6. Place the lobster halves, meat side down, on the hot grill and cook for 2 to 3 minutes.
7. Turn the lobster over and brush it with the remaining marinade and continue grilling for 3 to 5 minutes, or until the lobster meat is tender and white, not opaque.

MARINADE

1 clove garlic, minced
Juice of 1 lemon
2 Tbsp olive oil
1 tsp Old Bay Seasoning

1. In a small bowl, mix together all of the ingredients and set aside until needed.

Makes about 1/4 cup

COOKING FROZEN LOBSTER TAILS

To ensure that the meat is as tender as possible, thaw the frozen lobster tails in the refrigerator or put them in a sealable bag and set them under cold running water until thawed. Here are a few ways great ways to cook those tails.

Boiling

This is the easiest way to cook a lobster tail, but be sure not to overcook it. To prevent the tail from curling, stick a long metal skewer through it prior to boiling.

1. Bring a large stockpot of salted water to a boil over high heat. Add the lobster tail and boil, using the chart to guide you on timings. The lobster tail will turn bright red when it's cooked.
2. Using tongs, remove the tail from the pot when cooked.
3. To serve, crack open the tail, squeeze some lemon juice overtop, and dip in warm butter.

CHEAT SHEET

TAIL BOILING

Lobster Size	Cooking Time
¾ oz	4–5 minutes
⅚ oz	6 minutes
⅞ oz	7–8 minutes

Grilling

Next time you have company over, forget about steaks and pull out the lobster tails. Get them on the grill, sit back, and wait for the smiles.

1. As always, ensure the grill is clean. Using paper towel, wipe it with vegetable or canola oil to prevent the meat from sticking once it's hot. If you're cooking with charcoal, ensure that the coals are extremely hot. If you're cooking on a gas grill, set it to medium-high heat, 350°F–375°F.
2. Using a large, very sharp knife, cut the top of the shell lengthwise down the middle. Rub the tail meat with a fresh garlic clove and brush with melted butter.
3. Put the tails on the grill, shell side down.
4. Grill the lobster tails until the meat is white, juicy, and tender.
5. To serve, brush the grilled lobster tails with warm butter and olive oil, and season to taste with salt and pepper.

Baking

Try this method of cooking lobster tails next time you're camping or at the cottage in front of an open flame. An oven works just fine as well. Wrap the tail in aluminum foil, add a lemon wedge and some butter, and you're ready to go!

1. Preheat the oven to 400°F, or prepare your campfire, making sure you have an area of indirect heat available.
2. Using kitchen shears, cut the top shell off the lobster tail lengthwise to expose the meat.
3. Place the tail on a large sheet of aluminum foil. Season with kosher salt and freshly ground pepper, and add a lemon wedge and a dollop of butter. Wrap the foil tightly around the tail.

4. Bake for 7 to 8 minutes in the oven, or 4 minutes on the campfire over indirect heat (not in the flames). You want the tail meat to be nice and moist, so check it as it cooks to make sure it's not overdone.
5. To serve, top the tail with a chutney, salsa, or your favorite sauce.

Broiling

This is a great way to make a delicious lobster tail. Watch carefully as the tail can dry out quickly when it's broiled.

1. Preheat the broiler to high heat.
2. Using kitchen shears, cut the top shell off the lobster lengthwise.
3. Slightly separate the shell to expose the meat. Season the lobster meat with kosher salt and freshly ground black pepper.
4. Put the lobster tail on a baking sheet and broil for 7 to 8 minutes, or until the meat is white.
5. To serve, brush with your favorite sauce.

Steaming

This method makes for delicate, melt-in-your-mouth texture. You won't believe the flavor your lobster tails will have.

1. Add 2 inches of water and lots of kosher salt to a large pot. Place a steaming rack in the pot and bring the water to a rolling boil over high heat.
2. Lay the lobster tails in the pot, and cover quickly with a lid to trap the steam. Cook for 5 to 6 minutes. The lobster tails will turn bright red when cooked. Remove the tails with tongs.
3. To serve, break open the tail, squeeze some lemon juice overtop, and dip in warm butter.

{ HOW TO REMOVE THE MEAT FROM RAW LOBSTER }

A couple of the recipes require you to remove the meat from a lobster *before* it is cooked. To do this, you have to kill the lobster first. First, place the live lobster into the freezer for about 20 minutes. This will put the lobster into a catatonic state. Then, pierce a sharp knife directly through the top of the lobster's head (this will kill it instantly) and run it down through the center of the lobster's body to split it into two. Remove the meat as you would from a cooked lobster and rinse it very thoroughly under cold water. Uncooked lobster meat should be refrigerated in a covered bowl and used within 2 days. Note that lobster meat should not be eaten raw.

HOW TO EAT LOBSTER

Ah, the fun part! Now that your lobster is cooked through, you just have to
release the meat from its giant shell. Don't worry, it's not as complicated as it looks—you just
can't be shy. Grab your tools and get ready to dig in! I suggest kitchen shears,
a sharp knife, and a good, old-fashioned rolling pin for removing the deliciously sweet lobster
meat. And don't forget your bib! One last thing: remember that lobster meat is sweet and
tender when hot, and becomes less tender as it cools, so get in there fast!

CLAWS

Pull each claw off the lobster's body and use force to crack them with lobster crackers
or by smacking them with the back side of a large chef's knife. Dive in!

TAIL

Flip the tail upside down and use kitchen shears to cut the tissues connecting the meat
and shell. Be careful not to cut into the meat if you want to keep it in one piece.
Cut the tail in half to expose the meat and use kitchen shears to cut the connecting shell
on the bottom of the tail. Push the meat out in one piece.

KNUCKLES

Crack the knuckles with lobster crackers or a knife and use a lobster pick to push the meat out.

LEGS

If you want to eat lobster legs with class, do not suck the meat directly
out of the little legs. Instead, lay the legs on a flat work surface and use a rolling pin to
roll over each leg, pushing the meat out.

CORAL

Who doesn't love eating raw lobster eggs? Keep it simple and enjoy
eating them with a spoon. Or get creative and serve them on a cracker. You can also
remove them after a lobster has been cooked to use as a garnish.

TOMALLEY (LIVER)

Eat it raw or cooked by the spoonful or add it to sauces and stocks.

SHELLS

You don't want to eat these, but you do want to store them for later use. They're fantastic for
making an incredible lobster stock (page 186) or lobster butter (page 190).

BRUNCH

LOBSTER EGGS BENNY WITH TWO-STEP HOLLANDAISE SAUCE

Sunday, Sunday, Sunday . . . After a long Saturday night at one of our Rock Lobster restaurant locations, I'd love to sleep in on the Sunday morning, but that's not always possible. I don't usually have much time in the morning before heading to work, so a quick and easy recipe is my preference.

SERVES 4

Two-Step Hollandaise Sauce

4 egg yolks
1 Tbsp lemon juice
1 tsp Dijon mustard
Pinch of cayenne pepper
Kosher salt and freshly
   ground pepper
½ cup salted butter, melted

Eggs Benny

2 fresh frozen lobster tails,
   steamed and meat removed
   (see pages 21–23)
1 Tbsp white vinegar
Pinch of kosher salt
4 eggs
2 English muffins
4 slices peameal bacon
   (Canadian bacon)
3 chives, finely chopped
4–6 Tbsp Two-Step
   Hollandaise Sauce

1. For the sauce, in a food processor, combine the egg yolks, lemon juice, mustard, and cayenne pepper. Blend for 5 to 10 seconds. Season to taste with salt and pepper. With the machine running on high speed, pour the melted butter into the egg yolk mixture to thicken. If the sauce is too thick, slowly add 1 Tbsp of warm water at a time to the mixture and blend again. **2.** Transfer the sauce to a small saucepan and simmer, uncovered, over low heat to keep warm. Do not boil. **3.** Cut the lobster meat into large bite-sized pieces and place it in a bowl. **4.** For the eggs, fill a medium-sized saucepan with water to 3 inches deep and add the white vinegar and salt. Bring to a boil over high heat. Crack the eggs into the water, then turn off the heat immediately and let the eggs cook for 2 to 3 minutes, or until they float. When the eggs are done, remove them from the saucepan with a slotted spoon, and then place them on paper towel to dry if necessary. **5.** While the eggs are cooking, split the English muffins in two and toast them. While the muffins are toasting, heat a large frying pan to medium-high heat. Cook the bacon (no need to add oil) until crispy, then set on paper towel to absorb any excess fat. **6.** To serve, place a slice of bacon on top of each muffin half, then spoon on some lobster chunks. Add an egg on top of each one, then some sauce and a sprinkle of chopped chives.

Note: Feel free to swap the bacon for ham, smoked salmon, sliced shrimps, or thick-cut grilled tomatoes. The Hollandaise Sauce can be prepared in advance and refrigerated in an airtight container for up to 3 days.

LOBSTER CREPE WITH SWEET CARROT PUREE

This light sweet and savory dish is perfect for a nice little brunch. It also makes a great appetizer.

SERVES 4

Crepes
2 eggs
¾ cup flour
1 bunch chives, finely diced
2 Tbsp salted butter, melted
Kosher salt
1 cup milk

Filling
1 live lobster (about 1 ¼ lb),
   steamed and meat removed
   (see pages 17–23)
3 carrots, peeled
2 Tbsp unsalted butter
1 ½ tsp brown sugar
¼ cup white wine
1 shallot, finely diced
Kosher salt and freshly
   ground pepper
½ cup microgreens
   (pea shoots or micro basil)

1. For the crepes, whisk together the eggs, flour, chives, and butter with a pinch of salt in a large mixing bowl. Slowly pour in the milk while whisking. Continue to whisk until smooth. **2.** Heat a large nonstick frying pan over medium-high heat until hot, then pour a ladleful of crepe batter (about ¼ of the total batter) into the center of the pan. Lift the pan and roll the crepe mixture around so that it coats the entire bottom of the pan. Cook for 2 minutes over medium heat. Using a nonstick metal spatula, lift the edges of the crepe and carefully flip it. Cook for another 1 to 2 minutes, or until golden brown. Place the cooked crepe on a plate and allow to cool. **3.** Repeat with the remaining batter to make four crepes in total.
4. For the filling, cut the lobster meat into small pieces and place it in a mixing bowl. **5.** In a food processor, combine the carrots, butter, and brown sugar, and blend to a very smooth puree. Transfer the puree to a small saucepan.
6. In the mixing bowl, combine the lobster meat, white wine, and shallot with a pinch of salt and pepper. Mix well. Transfer to a separate small saucepan.
7. Heat both saucepans over medium heat for 2 minutes, or until the mixtures are heated through. Remove the lobster mixture from the heat. Continue to warm the carrot puree over low heat, stirring occasionally and taking care not to burn it.
8. Lay the crepes flat on a clean work surface and spoon 1 Tbsp of the lobster mixture directly onto the center of each one. Fold in the sides of each crepe to seal them. Flip them over so the seam sides are down. **9.** Evenly spoon the carrot puree into four shallow bowls, place a lobster crepe in the middle of each, and garnish with microgreens.

GREEN EGGS AND HAM LOBSTER SCRAMBLED EGGS

If you're like me, a big kid at heart, this recipe will remind you of your youth! This recipe comes from my favorite author as a child, the amazing Dr. Seuss. "Try them! Try them! And you may! Try them and you may, I say."

SERVES 4

1 live lobster (about 1 ¼ lb), steamed and meat removed (see pages 17–23)
8 eggs
¼ cup milk
2 small rounds cooked ham (about ½ lb in total), cut into ½-inch cubes
1 cup baby spinach
1 red bell pepper, finely diced
¼ cup shredded aged Cheddar cheese
Kosher salt and freshly ground pepper
1 Tbsp salted butter
Hot sauce
½ cup microgreens (pea shoots or micro basil)

1. Cut the lobster meat into medium-sized chunks. **2.** In a mixing bowl, whisk together the eggs and milk. Add the ham, spinach, bell pepper, cheese, and lobster meat. Season to taste with salt and pepper. **3.** In a large nonstick frying pan, melt the butter over low heat. Add the egg mixture to the pan and cook, stirring constantly, for 2 minutes, or until the eggs are cooked through. Be careful not to overcook them. **4.** Serve the scrambled eggs topped with a drizzle of your favorite hot sauce, the microgreens, and a few slices of toast.

Note: You can replace the cooked ham with pancetta or thick-cut smoked bacon.

DONNY'S LOBSTER BACON HASH

You may ask, who is Donny? My sous-chef? My general manager? Nope, it's Mr. P. himself, Don Juan Pettit, my dad. Since my father is of Irish decent, bacon hash made with lobster is the perfect tribute to him in this book.

SERVES 4

1 live lobster (about 1 ¼ lb), parboiled and meat removed, or 2 fresh frozen lobster tails, parboiled and meat removed (see pages 17–23)

4 large Yukon Gold or white potatoes, cut into ½-inch cubes

8 strips thick-cut bacon, chopped into ½-inch pieces

2 white onions, diced

1 large bulb fennel, diced

2 cloves garlic, minced

½ cup chicken stock

Smoked paprika

Kosher salt and freshly ground pepper

1 fresh Gala apple, cut into matchsticks

1. Chop the lobster meat into medium-sized chunks and place it in a bowl. **2.** Parboil the potatoes for 6 to 8 minutes. Drain and set aside. **3.** Line a plate with paper towel. **4.** In a large saucepan, fry the bacon pieces over medium-high heat until crispy. Remove them from the pan and place them on the prepared plate, leaving the fat in the pan. **5.** Return the pan to the heat, add the parboiled potatoes to the bacon fat, and cook for 5 minutes, or until soft and brown. Add the onions, fennel, and garlic and cook until soft, stirring constantly. Add the chicken stock to deglaze the pan, then turn down the heat to medium. Add the lobster meat and mix well to heat through. Add smoked paprika, salt, and pepper to taste. Stir well. **6.** Serve the hash on a plate topped with the bacon pieces and garnished with apple.

Note: For really awesome potatoes, cut them into cubes and leave them submerged overnight in a large saucepan or bowl of water before boiling them. This will take all the starch out of the potatoes, leaving them crunchy on the outside and soft in the middle when cooked.

THE KING'S LOBSTER GRILLED CHEESE

I created this recipe to say thanks to Darryl Fine, one of my partners. This guy is a living legend. One of his old restaurants, Shanghai Cowgirl, was a cornerstone of the Toronto food scene. It had a great run for over 13 years and was known for having the best grilled cheese in the city. It made perfect sense to me to bring back his grilled cheese—but with a delicious lobster twist.

SERVES 4

1 live lobster (about 1 ¼ lb), boiled and meat removed (see pages 17–23)
¼ cup salted butter, softened
8 slices sourdough bread
4 slices Havarti cheese
1 bunch fresh rosemary, finely chopped
4 pinches of truffle salt (found at gourmet specialty food stores)
4 slices smoked Gouda cheese

1. Cut the lobster meat into small pieces and place it in a bowl. **2.** Butter both sides of the bread slices, going right to the edges. **3.** Place a slice of Havarti cheese on the tops of four slices of the bread. Evenly spoon the lobster meat onto each slice, then sprinkle with rosemary and truffle salt. Top each with a slice of smoked Gouda cheese, and another slice of bread. **4.** In a large frying pan, fry the sandwiches, two at a time, over medium-high heat for 2 minutes on each side, or until they are golden brown on both sides and the cheese is melted. Repeat with the remaining two sandwiches. Serve immediately.

TOAD-IN-THE-HOLE

This recipe is an old-school brunch classic. In the UK, it's traditionally made with sausage and Yorkshire pudding mix, but in North America we know it as a slice of toast with the center cut out and an egg cooked in the middle. My mom used to make this for me (minus the lobster, sadly) as a fun way to eat eggs. If you have small kids, trust me, it works. You can thank me later!

SERVES 4

2 fresh frozen lobster tails, boiled, and meat removed (see pages 21–23)
2 Tbsp unsalted butter
4 small eggs, beaten
2 small shallots, finely diced
2 small jalapeño peppers, finely diced
Kosher salt and freshly ground pepper
4 slices thick-cut bread

1. Chop the lobster meat into bite-sized pieces. **2.** In a large frying pan, melt half of the butter over medium heat. **3.** In a mixing bowl, combine the eggs, shallots, and jalapeños with the lobster meat. Stir well and season to taste with salt and pepper. **4.** Using a small mug or cookie cutter, cut a hole out of the center of each slice of bread, about 2 inches in diameter. **5.** Place two slices of bread in the frying pan. Immediately spoon about 2 Tbsp of the egg-lobster mixture into each hole. Fry for 2 minutes without moving the bread. Using a nonstick metal spatula, carefully flip the bread and egg and continue to cook for 1 minute, or until the egg is cooked and the bread is toasted. Remove from the pan and keep warm in the oven until ready to serve. **6.** Melt the remaining butter in the frying pan and repeat with the remaining slices of bread and egg-lobster mixture. Serve immediately.

Note: Don't forget to fry the cut-out bread holes for an extra small bite!

ZE LOBSTER BLT

B (Bacon) + L (Lobster) + T (Tomato) = three amazing things combined together! All I know is that I really, really love this sandwich. If you like good things too, this quick and simple recipe may very well be for you. I like to serve these with dill pickles and kettle chips on the side.

SERVES 4

1 live lobster (about 1 ¼ lb), steamed and meat removed, or 2 fresh frozen lobster tails, steamed and meat removed (see pages 17–23)

½ cup mayonnaise

2 Tbsp lemon juice

2 tsp extra virgin olive oil

1 tsp Sriracha sauce

1 tsp finely chopped fresh tarragon

Kosher salt and freshly ground pepper

8 slices thick-cut bacon

4 ciabatta buns

2 Tbsp unsalted butter, softened

4 leaves Bibb lettuce

1 tomato, cut into 4 equal slices, with seeds

1. Cut the lobster meat into thick slices and place it in a bowl. **2.** In a separate large mixing bowl, combine the mayonnaise with the lemon juice, olive oil, Sriracha sauce, and tarragon. Season to taste with salt and pepper. Add the lobster meat slices and mix well. Cover and refrigerate until needed. **3.** Meanwhile, heat a large frying pan to medium-high. Cook the bacon (no need to add oil) until crispy, then set on paper towel to absorb any excess fat. **4.** Slice the buns in half and butter the insides. Lay one lettuce leaf and one slice of tomato in each bun, then top with the lobster mixture and two pieces of bacon. Cover with the top of the buns, cut them in half, and secure each half with a toothpick. **5.** Serve the sandwiches on individual plates with dill pickles and kettle chips.

Note: Feel free to use your favorite type of bread. You'll need toothpicks for this recipe.

SMALL PLATES

LOBSTER DEVILED EGGS

This dish is the reason I got this cookbook published! I was invited to be a participating chef at the Canadian Cookbook Awards in the fall of 2012, where I rocked this dish. I happened to meet my awesome soon-to-be publisher and the rest is history. (You have to start prepping this recipe about 4 hours in advance.)

SERVES 6

6 beets
1 Tbsp olive oil
1 live lobster (about 1 ¼ lb),
    boiled and meat removed
    (see pages 17–23)
6 eggs
1 Tbsp white vinegar
1 tsp kosher salt
2 Tbsp mayonnaise
1 Tbsp Dijon mustard
1 tsp smoked paprika
Kosher salt and freshly
    ground pepper
1 bunch chives, finely
    chopped

1. Preheat the oven to 400°F. In a bowl, toss the beets in the 1 Tbsp of olive oil, season to taste with salt and pepper, and wrap in aluminum foil. Bake for 2 hours, or until soft. **2.** Remove the beets from the oven and peel while hot. Cut each beet into quarters and set in a bowl of ice water for 2 hours. **3.** Finely chop the lobster meat and place it in a bowl. **4.** In a heavy 3-quart saucepan, cover the eggs with 3 inches of cold water, then add the vinegar and salt. Partially cover the saucepan and bring the water to a rolling boil. Cook for 8 to 10 minutes. Remove from the heat and let stand, covered, for 10 minutes. **5.** Transfer the eggs to a bowl of ice water to stop the cooking process. Let stand for 5 minutes. **6.** Peel the eggs and cut them in half lengthwise. Using a spoon, carefully remove the yolks and place them in a bowl. Carefully place the whites in the beet juice bowl. Mash the yolks with the back of a fork, and add the mayonnaise, mustard, and smoked paprika. Stir until smooth. Season to taste with salt and pepper. **7.** Place the yolk mixture in a food processor and add the chopped lobster meat. Blend until smooth. **8.** Place the lobster-egg mixture in a piping bag or a small sealable plastic bag with one bottom corner snipped off. Pipe some lobster-egg mixture into each egg-white half. Garnish with chives and serve immediately.

Note: The longer you keep the egg whites in the beet juice, the richer and more amazing the dark purple/reddish color will be. If you're in a hurry, you can buy a jar of sliced beets and soak the egg whites in that liquid instead of roasting whole beets.

LOBSTER CROQUETTES

My original Rock Lobster restaurant is located in a very cool area of Toronto—what used to be the heart of Little Portugal. This recipe came to me from my frequent cravings for cod croquettes from the old Portuguese bakery down the street.

SERVES 4

Matty's Seafood Sauce
   (page 186)
1 live lobster (about 1 ¼ lb),
   boiled and meat removed
   (see pages 17–23)
½ cup white wine
2 tsp Old Bay Seasoning
   (or your favorite seafood
   seasoning)
Kosher salt
1 ½ cups dried Italian
   breadcrumbs
3 Tbsp salted butter, softened
3 eggs
2 green onions, finely diced
1 shallot, finely diced
Juice of 1 lemon
Vegetable oil (for frying)

1. Prepare the Matty's Seafood Sauce. **2.** Finely chop the lobster meat and place it in a bowl. **3.** In a large frying pan, combine 3 cups of water with the white wine, 1 tsp of the seafood seasoning, and salt to taste. Bring to a boil over high heat. Turn down the heat to medium and add the lobster meat. Simmer for 4 to 5 minutes. **4.** In a large mixing bowl, combine the lobster mixture with the remaining 1 tsp of the seafood seasoning, breadcrumbs, butter, eggs, green onions, shallot, and lemon juice, and stir well. Cover and place in the refrigerator for 30 minutes to allow the flavors to develop. **5.** Line a baking sheet with parchment paper. **6.** Using your hands, form the lobster mixture into a large ball and then roll it out into a long tube shape, about 1 inch in diameter. Using a sharp knife, cut the mixture into 1 ½-inch-long pieces and transfer to the prepared baking sheet. Wrap the baking sheet tightly in plastic wrap, seal, and refrigerate for a minimum of 2 hours and a maximum of 24 hours. **7.** Line a plate with paper towel. **8.** In a large cast-iron frying pan, heat ½ inch of vegetable oil over medium-high heat. **9.** Place the lobster croquettes in the frying pan four at a time and cook, flipping once with a nonstick metal spatula, for 2 to 4 minutes or until golden brown. **10.** Transfer the croquettes to the prepared plate to soak up any excess oil. **11.** Serve with Matty's Seafood Sauce on the side.

Note: You can easily swap the lobster meat for cod, halibut, salmon, or shrimp.

ALL LOBSTER "NO CRAB" CAKES WITH OLD BAY AIOLI

They say Maryland does two things well: play football and make crab cakes! Maryland classic crab cakes have been a part of my diet for a number of years, and when I opened Rock Lobster I knew I had to have a lobster version. Of course, you can use crab instead of lobster for these cakes, but I wouldn't.

SERVES 4

Seafood Seasoning Aioli
  (page 191)
1 live lobster (about 1 ¼ lb),
  boiled and meat removed
  (see pages 17–23)
1 bunch chives, minced
¼ cup mayonnaise
1 egg
1 Tbsp Old Bay Seasoning
  (or your favorite seafood
  seasoning)
2 tsp Dijon mustard
½ cup panko breadcrumbs
1 cup baby arugula
1 lemon, sliced

1. Prepare the Seafood Seasoning Aioli. **2.** Roughly chop the lobster meat and place it in a bowl. **3.** In a large bowl, combine the chives, mayonnaise, egg, seafood seasoning, and mustard, and mix well with a fork. Add the chopped lobster meat and ¼ cup of the breadcrumbs, and continue mixing. Using your hands, form the lobster-breadcrumb mixture into four 2-inch-wide cakes. **4.** On a large work surface, lay out the remaining ¼ cup of the breadcrumbs. Finish the cakes by rolling them in the breadcrumbs. **5.** Place the lobster cakes directly on a baking sheet and chill, uncovered, in the refrigerator for 25 to 30 minutes. **6.** Preheat the oven to 375°F. **7.** Bake the lobster cakes for 15 minutes, or until golden brown. **8.** To serve, lay the baby arugula on a large serving dish and place the lobster cakes on top. Top each cake with dollop of Seafood Seasoning Aioli and serve immediately, with the lemon slices on the side.

Note: If you prefer, you can fry the cakes for a nice added crunch. Just heat 1 Tbsp of vegetable or canola oil in a deep frying pan over medium-high heat, and fry the cakes for 2 minutes per side.

DANA'S LOBSTER CUCUMBER CROSTINI

Almost as easy as 1, 2, 3. This is the ultimate versatile dish: perfect for a dinner party appetizer or a Wednesday night snack on the couch with a beer in hand. It's best served cold.

SERVES 6

3 Tbsp Sriracha Mayo
(page 191)
1 live lobster (about 1 ¼ lb),
    boiled and meat removed,
    or 2 fresh frozen lobster tails,
    boiled and meat removed
    (see pages 17–23)
1 lemon
2 tsp Old Bay Seasoning
    (or your favorite seafood
    seasoning)
1 English cucumber

1. Prepare the Sriracha Mayo. **2.** Chop the lobster meat into chunks and place it in a medium-sized bowl. Squeeze the lemon over the lobster to cover it in juice and then sprinkle with the seafood seasoning. Cover and place in the refrigerator to chill for at least 30 minutes and no more than 6 hours, as the citrus will cook the lobster meat. **3.** Meanwhile, cut the cucumber into ½-inch-thick slices and place them in the refrigerator to keep cold. **4.** When ready to serve, place the cold cucumber pieces on a serving plate and top each one with lobster meat. Garnish with a drizzle of Sriracha Mayo.

LOBSTER ARANCINI

I have a favorite little Italian restaurant in Toronto called Sotto Voce that makes an amazing arancini (rice balls filled with meat and red sauce), so of course I had to try my own version with a lobstah spin. Preparing this dish can take some time, but I promise you that it's worth the effort. I like to serve these with Matty's Seafood Sauce (page 186).

SERVES 4

1 live lobster (about 1 ¼ lb), boiled and meat removed (see pages 17–23), cooking broth reserved and kept warm
1 Tbsp unsalted butter
1 Tbsp vegetable oil
1 cup Arborio rice
½ cup white wine
¼ cup chicken stock
1 Tbsp extra virgin olive oil
1 head garlic, minced
1 tomato, diced
2 fresh basil leaves, finely chopped
½ cup grated Parmigiano-Reggiano cheese
½ cup shredded aged Cheddar cheese
1 cup flour
2 eggs, beaten
1 cup dried Italian breadcrumbs
¼ cup canola or vegetable oil
Kosher salt and finely ground pepper

1. In a medium-sized saucepan, heat the butter and vegetable oil over medium heat. Add the Arborio rice and cook for 2 minutes. **2.** Stir in the white wine (this will help pull the flavor out of the rice). Continue stirring as you add ½ cup of the reserved lobster broth. Keep stirring until the broth is completely absorbed. Repeat, adding ½ cup of the lobster broth at a time, until the rice becomes very thick and creamy (you'll probably need about 4 cups in total, but use more if necessary). The process will take 25 to 30 minutes. Once the rice is cooked, remove it from the heat and set aside to cool. **3.** Dice the lobster meat and place it in a large saucepan. Add the chicken stock and olive oil, then the garlic, tomato, basil, and both cheeses. Simmer, uncovered, for 15 to 20 minutes, or until thickened. **4.** Place the flour in one bowl, eggs in another bowl, and breadcrumbs in a third bowl. **5.** To prepare the rice balls, wet your hands with water and scoop up a small handful (about 3 Tbsp) of cooked rice. Place 1 tsp of the lobster mixture in the center of the rice and top with another 1 Tbsp of the rice. Using your hands, seal the ball by packing the rice tightly together and then rolling it in the flour. Repeat with the remaining rice mixture. **6.** Place the balls directly on a baking sheet and allow them to set for 30 minutes at room temperature. **7.** Roll the balls in the beaten egg and then the breadcrumbs. Return them to the baking sheet until you're ready to fry them. **8.** In a medium-sized pot, heat a thin layer of oil over medium-high heat. Add the balls to the pan and roll them around in the hot oil until browned on all sides (this happens very quickly, so be careful). The balls will warm through to their center as they fry. Place them on paper towel to absorb any excess oil, and season to taste with salt and pepper. **9.** Serve the hot fried rice balls on a platter with your favorite sauce (or tomato sauce) for dipping.

Note: Keep the lobster broth (from when you boil the lobster) for cooking the Arborio rice. The arancini can be prepared up to 6 hours ahead of time and refrigerated until you are ready to fry them.

LOBSTER, CREAM CHEESE, AND CHIVE PUFF PASTRIES

Warm bread, soft cheese, and lobster all wrapped together. Perfection, if you ask me. Grab a beer and enjoy!

SERVES 4 TO 6

1 live lobster (about 1 ¼ lb), boiled and meat removed (see pages 17–23)

1 cup cream cheese

2 shallots, finely diced

1 bunch chives, finely chopped

Kosher salt and freshly ground pepper

½ cup flour (for dusting)

½ lb puff pastry, partially thawed (see Note)

1 egg, beaten

1. Chop the lobster meat into large pieces and place it in a mixing bowl. Add the cream cheese, shallots, and chives. Mix together using a fork, and season to taste with salt and pepper. Set aside. **2.** Preheat the oven to 400°F. **3.** On a large, floured working surface, unfold the partially thawed pastry. Using a rolling pin, roll out the pastry into long pieces, about ¼ inch thick. Cut the pastry into ½-inch-wide strips (you should get 6 to 7 strips). **4.** Using a spoon, form the lobster mixture into as many balls as you have pastry strips and place one at the top of each pastry strip. Roll the pastry strip around the lobster mixture until it is tight. Seal the edges with your thumbs. Repeat with the remaining pastry strips and lobster mixture. **5.** Place the pastries on a baking sheet and brush them all over with the beaten egg. Bake for 12 to 15 minutes, or until the crust is golden brown. Serve immediately.

Note: You can use store-bought puff pastry for this to make life easier. Remove frozen puff pastry from the freezer to partially thaw for 10 to 15 minutes before you plan to use it. Do not completely thaw it as it will become very sticky and difficult to fold.

DEEP-FRIED LOBSTER WONTONS WITH PONZU SAUCE

I remember day trips with my parents to Kensington Market in Toronto. That's where I got my first sense of Asian culture—and I've been hooked ever since. This recipe uses Ponzu Sauce, which is a simple citrus-soy sauce, but you could also dip the lobster wontons in a sweet and sour sauce or spicy Sriracha Mayo (page 191).

SERVES 4

Ponzu Sauce (page 189)
1 live lobster (about 1 ¼ lb), parboiled and meat removed (see pages 17–23)
2 green onions, finely diced
1 clove garlic, minced
1 tsp freshly grated ginger
1 Tbsp lemon juice
12 wonton wrappers
¼ cup cornstarch
1 cup canola or vegetable oil

1. Prepare the Ponzu Sauce. **2.** Chop the lobster meat into small pieces and place it in a bowl. Set aside. **3.** In a separate bowl, combine the green onions, garlic, and ginger with the lemon juice. Stir well. Add the lobster meat and mix well until everything binds together nicely. Set aside. **4.** Place the 12 wontons on a cutting board and brush their edges with water. Place ½ Tbsp lobster filling on each wonton and seal the edges of each to form a triangle. **5.** Dust a large plate with cornstarch and lightly roll the wontons in the cornstarch. This will seal them and will prevent them from sticking to each other. **6.** Line a plate with paper towel. **7.** In a medium-sized saucepan, warm the oil (it should be about 1 ½ to 2 inches deep) over medium-high heat. Fry the wontons in batches until they begin to float and are golden brown and crispy. Do not overcrowd the saucepan. Transfer them to the prepared plate. **8.** Serve immediately with the Ponzu Sauce for dipping.

DEEP-FRIED LOBSTER CHEESE BALLS

I remember eating, as a kid, deep-fried cheese balls at my friend's birthday party at the local bowling alley. I could never have imagined that years later I would be trying to make them ghetto-gourmet!

SERVES 4

1 live lobster (about 1 ¼ lb), boiled and meat removed (see pages 17–23)
½ cup shredded Cheddar cheese
1 cup cream cheese
3 Tbsp mayonnaise
1 Tbsp Old Bay Seasoning (or your favorite seafood seasoning)
½ cup flour
½ cup buttermilk
½ cup dried Italian breadcrumbs
Canola oil (for frying)

1. Finely chop the lobster meat and place it in a bowl. **2.** In the same bowl, add the Cheddar cheese, cream cheese, mayonnaise, and seafood seasoning, and mix well. Using your hands, roll the mixture into 8 to 12 small balls. Place them on a plate or baking sheet, cover with plastic wrap, and refrigerate for 1 hour. **3.** Put the flour, buttermilk, and breadcrumbs in three separate bowls. Take each lobster ball in turn and roll it in the flour, then the buttermilk, then the breadcrumbs. **4.** In a small pot, warm 2 to 3 inches of the canola oil over high heat. When the oil is very hot and slightly bubbling, fry the lobster balls in batches for 1 to 2 minutes, or until golden brown. Place the balls on paper towel to absorb any excess oil. Serve immediately.

LOBSTER BRUSCHETTA

This is another Italian-inspired lobstah dish. I have had some amazing trips to Italy over the years and this type of recipe brings back fond memories. It may not be a classic recipe but it is certainly a lot of fun.

1. Chop the lobster meat into bite-sized pieces and place it in a large bowl. Set aside. **2.** Using a knife, scrape the kernels off each corn cob into a bowl. Set aside. **3.** Cut the baguette into rounds. Drizzle the rounds with olive oil, season to taste with salt and pepper, and lightly toast. **4.** Combine the lobster meat with the avocado cubes, diced tomatoes, celery, corn kernels, mayonnaise, and chilis. Mix well. **5.** Lay out the toasted bread rounds. Evenly spoon lobster mixture onto each round and garnish with finely chopped chives. Serve cold.

Note: I prefer this served cold. If you prefer it warm, you can quickly heat the lobster mixture in a frying pan over medium heat before putting it on the bread.

SERVES 4 TO 6

1 live lobster (about 1 ¼ lb),
   boiled and meat removed
   (see pages 17–23)
2 ears fresh corn, cooked
1 medium baguette
Extra virgin olive oil
Kosher salt and freshly
   ground pepper
1 avocado, cut into
   ½-inch cubes
3 on-the-vine tomatoes,
   finely diced
½ cup roughly chopped celery
½ cup mayonnaise
1 Tbsp bird's eye (Thai) chilis,
   thinly sliced
¼ cup finely chopped chives

Bymark's Lobster Poutine
Chef Mark McEwan (Bymark)

Lobster poutine has been a staple at Bymark, a restaurant in the financial district of Toronto, for years. The first incarnation of the dish came after a busy dinner service. My staff and I were cleaning up and decided to make a late-night snack with some of the ingredients that were left over. We had béarnaise, lobster, and fries. After our first bite, we knew we were on to something. We fine-tuned the recipe, and ever since then it has been the talk of the town and a must-have when dining at Bymark.

Note: This recipe makes ¾ cup of gastrique. Store the leftover gastrique in an airtight container in the refrigerator for up to 1 month. Warm it up and use it in place of gravy.

1. To prepare the french fries, trim one side of the potatoes so that they sit flat and stable on the cutting board. Slice them into the desired french fry size and plunge them in ice-cold water. Soak for a few hours at least, ideally overnight, changing the water every 4 hours or so. **2.** For the gastrique, combine the white wine, red wine vinegar, shallots, bay leaves, salt, sugar, and peppercorns in a saucepan. Bring to a boil, uncovered, then simmer gently on low heat to reduce by half, 12 to 15 minutes. Strain through a fine mesh sieve and let cool. **3.** For the béarnaise sauce, heat the 1 cup of clarified butter in a saucepan to 120°F to melt. **4.** Place a stainless-steel mixing bowl over a pot of simmering water, add the egg yolks and 1 Tbsp of the gastrique, and whisk them together until the mixture thickens and turns pale yellow, 4 to 8 minutes. **5.** Remove the

Note: Lobster Shell Basket: Preheat the oven to 400°F. Using sharp kitchen shears, trim the semi-translucent underside from the tail shell, discard, and then cut the hard shell in half lengthwise. Rinse well and shake dry. Puncture a hole in each shell half near the broad top of the tail and then through its tail fan. Tie the halves together, tail fan to top of tail, with the top of the shell facing outward to create a basket. Place the shell basket on a baking sheet, brush with melted butter, and roast in the oven until dry and fragrant, 10 to 12 minutes.

SERVES 2

French Fries
2 large Yukon Gold potatoes
   (about 1 ¼ lb combined)
8 cups vegetable or canola oil
Salt

Gastrique
1 cup white wine
½ cup red wine vinegar
2 shallots, sliced
2 bay leaves
2 tsp kosher salt
1 tsp granulated sugar
1 tsp black peppercorns

Béarnaise Sauce
1 cup Clarified Butter
   (page 189)
2 egg yolks
1 Tbsp gastrique
½ tsp lemon juice
3 drops of Tabasco sauce
3 drops of Worcestershire sauce
1 Tbsp chopped fresh tarragon
Salt and freshly ground
   white pepper
1 Tbsp chopped chives

Lobster
1 live lobster, about 1 ¼
   lb, parboiled and meat
   removed (see pages 17–23),
   tail shell reserved
1 cup Clarified Butter
   (page 189)

bowl from the heat, and, whisking constantly, slowly add the melted butter. Add the lemon juice, Tabasco and Worcestershire sauces, tarragon, and salt and pepper to taste. Cover the saucepan with a clean kitchen towel and place it on the stovetop to keep the béarnaise warm from the latent heat of the burner. You should avoid direct heat at this stage. **6.** For the lobster, cut the lobster meat into bite-sized pieces. Heat the remaining 1 cup of the clarified butter to 120°F to melt it. Be careful not to let it boil. Add the lobster meat pieces to the melted butter. **7.** When you are ready to begin cooking the french fries, heat the oil in a deep-fryer or deep saucepan to 325°F. Dry the french fries thoroughly with a towel and then blanch them in the hot oil until they wilt, 4 to 7 minutes. Remove them from the oil and drain on paper towel. Increase the heat of the oil to 400°F. Fry the blanched french fries until bronzed and crisp, 3 to 5 minutes. Drain, then toss with lashings of salt. **8.** If you're using the lobster basket (see Note), place it in the center of a serving plate. Otherwise, simply scatter some of the chives over a warm serving plate. Add half of the fries, then half of the lobster and dab with béarnaise. Add another layer of fries, the remaining lobster, the remaining béarnaise, and finally, the remaining chives.

RLFC LOBSTER POUTINE

Being Canadian, I have eaten many varieties of the Quebec gem, poutine—from foie gras, to bison, to cheeseburger flavor. It's safe to say I love the stuff! It's one of my favorite treats and, of course, lobster makes it that much better. Kick your poutine up a notch with the King of the Sea, and no doubt it will impress your friends. (You have to start prepping this recipe a day in advance.)

1. Prepare the Lobster Cappuccino Bisque. **2.** Scrub and clean the potatoes. Cut them into long rectangular pieces for fries. Submerge the cut potatoes in water to pull all the starch from them. Do this overnight (aim for 12 to 24 hours). **3.** Fill a deep-fryer or a deep saucepan with 3 inches of vegetable oil. Heat the oil to 350°F, then blanch the fries for a few minutes to partially cook them (see Note). Remove them from the fryer (or saucepan) and dry with paper towel. Leave the oil in the deep-fryer or saucepan, but turn off the heat. **4.** In a small bowl, whisk the cornstarch with ½ cup water. **5.** In a small saucepan, bring the bisque to a boil over high heat. Turn down the heat to a simmer and add the cornstarch mixture. Whisk until well combined and simmer, uncovered, for 2 to 3 minutes. **6.** Roughly chop the lobster meat, place it in a bowl, and set aside. **7.** When ready for final cooking, bring the oil back to 350°F and cook the fries for 1 to 2 minutes to finish them off. **8.** Place the cooked fries in a large serving bowl and sprinkle them with sea salt to taste. Top with cheese curds and lobster bisque. Add the chopped lobster meat and garnish with chopped chives. Serve immediately.

Note: Blanching the fries first will make them nice and crispy on the outside, soft and delicious on the inside.

SERVES 4

¾ cup Lobster Cappuccino Bisque (page 84)
6 large Yukon Gold potatoes
Vegetable oil (for frying)
1 Tbsp cornstarch
1 live lobster (about 1 ¼ lb), boiled and meat removed (see pages 17–23)
Sea salt
2 cups Quebec cheese curds or mozzarella, cut into bite-sized pieces
1 bunch chives, chopped

LOBSTER NACHOS

I tried this dish for the first time in Los Cabos, Mexico, and needed to take the idea home with me. I think you'll love my fresh, tasty version of this recipe.

1. Chop the lobster meat into medium-sized pieces and place it in a mixing bowl. Add the avocados, shallots, tomato, and bell peppers with ½ cup of the cilantro and the lime juice. Season to taste with salt and pepper. Mix well. Cover and place in the refrigerator to keep cool. **2.** In a mixing bowl, combine the sour cream and Sriracha sauce. Mix well and set aside. **3.** On a large plate, stack the tortilla chips and top them with the chilled lobster-avocado mixture. Garnish the chips with the remaining ½ cup of the cilantro and drizzle the sour cream–Sriracha sauce mixture overtop.

SERVES 2 TO 4

1 live lobster (about 1 ¼ lb),
    boiled and meat removed
    (see pages 17–23)
2 large ripe avocados,
    cut into 1-inch cubes
2 shallots, finely diced
1 large tomato, diced
1 yellow bell pepper, diced
    into ½-inch pieces
1 green bell pepper, diced
    into ½-inch pieces
1 cup chopped cilantro
Juice of 1 lime
Kosher salt and freshly
    ground pepper
¼ cup sour cream
1 Tbsp Sriracha sauce
5 big handfuls tortilla chips

Note: If you want to make your own tortilla chips, preheat the oven to 400°F. Cut fresh corn or flour tortillas into quarters. Place them on a baking sheet, drizzle with olive oil, and sprinkle with salt. Bake for 5 to 7 minutes, or until golden brown and crisp.

PEPPER'S LOBSTER, CRAB, AND CHEESE DIP

I'm sure you've seen a lobster or crab dip at your favorite chain restaurant, but I'm willing to bet you've never seen one like this. Break this dish out if you're looking to impress your friends and family. (And in case you're wondering who Pepper is, I got the nickname Pepper from my good friend Ian MacInnis while I was in university. It's not a story that's suitable for this book, but let's just say, I will not be eating another extremely insane hot ghost pepper any time soon!)

SERVES 4 TO 6

1 live lobster (about 1 ¼ lb), boiled and meat removed (see pages 17–23)

2 clusters cooked frozen Atlantic snow crab (about 1 lb in total)

1 cup cream cheese

2 cups baby spinach, roughly chopped

1 bunch green onions, thinly sliced

½ cup salted butter, melted

2 tsp Old Bay Seasoning (or your favorite seafood seasoning)

Pinch of cayenne pepper

1 tsp capers, finely diced

3 drops of Worcestershire sauce

½ cup panko breadcrumbs

½ cup shredded aged Cheddar cheese

1 baguette

1. Cut the lobster meat into medium-sized cubes and place it in a bowl. Set aside. **2.** Bring a large saucepan of salted water to a boil over high heat. Submerge the cooked frozen snow crab for 2 to 3 minutes to thaw. Remove the crab from the saucepan. Using kitchen shears, crack the shell and remove the crab meat. Set aside in a bowl. **3.** Preheat the oven to 375°F. **4.** In a mixing bowl, combine the cream cheese, baby spinach, and green onions with the melted butter, seafood seasoning, cayenne pepper, capers, Worcestershire sauce, half of the lobster meat, and all of the crab meat. Using a wooden spoon, mix all the ingredients together until thoroughly combined. **5.** Spoon the dip mixture into a large casserole dish and sprinkle with the breadcrumbs and cheese. Bake, covered, for 30 to 35 minutes, or until golden brown and bubbling. **6.** Cut the bread into bite-sized cubes. Place on a baking sheet and toast in the oven until brown. (This will only take a few minutes, so watch the bread in case it starts to burn.) **7.** Stick toothpicks in the remaining lobster cubes and in the toast cubes. Serve them alongside the warm dip.

Note: A crab cluster means one whole crab with its center, knuckles, and legs (this recipe calls for two).

LOBSICLE WITH SRIRACHA MAYO

I am a big fan of *any* food on a stick. Every summer I love to visit a variety of fairs and festivals in the USA. It's great to see the different food vendors trying to outdo each another with what they can serve on a stick! I started making these Lobsicles at our second pop-up event, and they've been a huge hit ever since. Large shrimp also work well.

SERVES 4

Sriracha Mayo (page 191)
4 fresh frozen lobster tails,
    boiled (see page 21)
1 cup panko breadcrumbs
1 tsp cayenne pepper
Kosher salt and freshly
    ground pepper
2 eggs
2 cups canola oil
2 lemons

1. Prepare the Sriracha Mayo. **2.** Remove the lobster meat, in one piece, from each tail and place it on a plate (see page 23). Cover and refrigerate until needed. **3.** In a shallow bowl, gently mix the breadcrumbs with the cayenne pepper and a pinch of salt and pepper. Beat the eggs in a separate shallow bowl. **4.** Line a large plate with paper towel. **5.** Take one piece of lobster tail meat at a time and dip it completely into the beaten egg and then into the seasoned breadcrumbs. Insert a wooden skewer or chopstick into the bottom of the lobster piece. Lay it on the paper towel to remove any excess liquid. Repeat with the remaining lobster tail meat pieces. **6.** Add 2 inches of canola oil to a deep medium-sized saucepan. Heat the oil over high heat to 350°F. When the oil is hot and slightly bubbling, submerge and cook one lobster tail at a time for 1 to 2 minutes, or until the lobster tail floats. The oil will be very hot, so be careful and watch that the lobster tail doesn't burn. Place the deep-fried tail on the prepared plate to absorb any excess oil. Repeat with the remaining tails. **7.** Season the lobster tails to taste with salt. Serve on a plate with a lemon half for squeezing and Sriracha Mayo for dipping.

LOBSTER CORN DAWGS

This dish is a good follow-up to the last recipe, Lobsicle—I told you, I love any food on a stick! This is such a fun dish. I like to dip these corn dawgs into my Matty's Seafood Sauce (page 186) or a hot Dijon mustard and mayonnaise mixture. Adding cooked shrimp or crab meat to the lobster meat will make them seafood corn dawgs!

SERVES 4

Corn Dawgs

1 live lobster (about 1 ¼ lb), boiled and meat removed (see pages 17–23)
½ cup heavy cream
¼ cup mayonnaise
2 sprigs fresh tarragon, finely chopped
1 tsp cayenne pepper
Kosher salt and freshly ground pepper
3 cups canola oil (for frying)

Batter

2 cups yellow cornmeal
1 cup flour
1 tsp baking soda
Kosher salt
2 cups milk
2 eggs
Canola oil
¼ cup cornstarch (for dredging)

1. For the corn dawgs, finely chop the lobster meat and place in the bowl of a food processor. Add the cream, mayonnaise, tarragon, and cayenne pepper. Puree until smooth. Add salt and pepper to taste. **2.** Spoon the lobster mixture into a piping bag that has a ½-inch-wide end piece. If you do not have a piping bag, use a sealable plastic bag with one of the bottom corners cut off to about ½ inch wide. **3.** On a flat work surface, lay out a large sheet of plastic wrap and pipe a line of lobster mixture (5 inches long x ½ inch thick) onto the plastic wrap. Wrap the meat mixture several times in the plastic and seal by twisting both ends. **4.** Cut the mixture into lobster "links" about 3 inches long and stick a Popsicle stick in the end of each one. **5.** Lay the lobster links directly on a baking sheet and place in the freezer for 1 hour to set. **6.** Meanwhile, prepare the batter. Combine the 2 cups of cornmeal, flour, baking soda, and a pinch of salt in a large bowl. Mix together. Add the milk and eggs and, using a wooden spoon, mix well to create the batter. Set aside. **7.** Line a plate with paper towel. **8.** Add 2 inches of canola oil to a deep medium-sized saucepan. Heat the oil over high heat to 350°F. **9.** Remove the lobster links from the freezer. Discard the plastic wrap and dip one link at a time in the cornstarch and then the batter. Place the battered link in the hot oil for 3 to 5 minutes, or until golden brown. Place on the prepared plate to absorb any excess oil. Repeat with the remaining links. Serve immediately with your favorite dipping sauce.

BEER-BATTERED BUFFALO LOBSTER POPCORN

I am a huge NFL fan and I love to show Sunday game day at both Rock Lobster restaurants. Being a seafood house, we don't make chicken wings, but I thought of the next best thing: beer-battered buffalo lobster popcorn. I'm a huge Buffalo Bills fan! I like to use Samuel Adams Boston Lager for the batter and Matty's Seafood Sauce (page 186), blue cheese dressing, or ranch dressing for dipping.

SERVES 4 TO 6

2 live lobsters (about 1 ¼ lb each), parboiled and meat removed (see pages 17–23)
1 bottle (355 ml) lager
1 cup flour
1 tsp baking soda
1 tsp salt
½ cup canola oil
½ cup salted butter
¼ cup hot sauce
2 carrots, peeled and cut into evenly sized sticks
2 stalks celery, cut into evenly sized sticks
Dipping sauces

1. Cut the lobster meat into bite-sized pieces and place it in a bowl. Set aside. **2.** In a large bowl, combine the beer, flour, baking soda, and salt. Using a whisk, beat until the batter is smooth. **3.** Line a plate with paper towel. **4.** Heat 2 inches of canola oil in a medium-sized saucepan over high heat to 350°F. **5.** Dip the lobster meat pieces in the batter, ensuring they are completely covered. **6.** Deep-fry the battered lobster pieces for 1 to 2 minutes in the hot oil, or until golden brown. Place the lobster popcorn on the prepared plate to absorb any excess oil. **7.** In a separate saucepan, melt the butter over medium heat. Add the hot sauce and heat the mixture until warmed through. **8.** In a large mixing bowl, toss the lobster popcorn with the warm hot sauce mixture to coat. Serve with the cut carrots, celery, and a variety of sauces for dipping.

SURF 'N' TURF STEAK TARTARE WITH VANILLA BUTTER POACHED LOBSTER

SERVES 8

1 live lobster (about 1 ¼ lb),
   steamed and meat removed
   (see pages 17–23)
1 lb beef tenderloin (center cut)
1 egg yolk
4 small anchovy fillets
⅓ cup capers, drained
⅓ cup cornichons, drained
¼ cup minced fresh flat-leaf
   parsley
2 Tbsp Dijon mustard
2 tsp Worcestershire sauce
Kosher salt and freshly
   ground pepper
¼ cup canola oil
¼ cup salted butter
1 vanilla bean, split in two
   and seeded (seeds reserved)
4 cups salted kettle chips

Having tried countless variations of steak tartare, I've come to the conclusion that my recipe is my personal favorite! Make sure to ask your butcher for his or her best tenderloin to ensure the freshest meat. Feel free to add your own personal twist by adding jalapeños or fried onion strings, or skip the meat altogether and use vegetables instead.

1. Cut the lobster meat into large bite-sized pieces and place it in a bowl. Set aside. **2.** Slice the beef tenderloin into very thin pieces and then dice. Transfer the beef to a bowl, cover with plastic wrap, and refrigerate until needed. **3.** In a food processor, combine the egg yolk, anchovies, capers, cornichons, parsley, mustard, and Worcestershire sauce. Pulse until finely chopped. Season to taste with salt and pepper. With the machine running, slowly add the oil until emulsified. You are looking for a thick mixture that will help bind the meat together later. Transfer to a medium-sized bowl and set aside. **4.** In a small saucepan, bring the butter and vanilla bean seeds to a simmer over low heat. Add the lobster meat and cook for 2 to 3 minutes, or until completely heated through and evenly coated with vanilla butter. Remove from the heat and set aside. **5.** Remove the diced beef tenderloin from the refrigerator and add it to the egg yolk mixture. Mix well to create the tartare. **6.** Using a 2-inch mold, place a small mound of tartare in the center of each of eight plates. Press the tartare firmly into the mold. Gently remove the mold and top the steak with the vanilla butter–coated lobster meat. Serve with kettle chips on the side.

LOBSTER CARPACCIO

Here's my take on a classic Italian dish that traditionally uses very thin slices of meat. My version uses lobster, of course, and is a great combination of flavors, with the citrus and ginger adding that something special. So delicious!

1. Slice the whole pieces of tail meat into ¼-inch-thick medallions and cut the claw meat into ¼-inch-thick slices. **2.** Place the lobster meat on a serving plate and drizzle with the Yuzu juice. **3.** In a small saucepan, heat the sesame oil over high heat. Drizzle the hot oil all over the lobster to cook the thin meat, turning the meat to ensure it's all coated. Cut the green apple into matchsticks. Garnish the lobster with the apple, chives, and ginger. Top with fresh lemon zest and microgreens.

Note: Yuzu juice is a very tart Japanese citrus juice. If you are looking to reduce your costs, feel free to replace it with a mix of equal parts fresh lemon and lime juice.

SERVES 4

2 live lobsters (about 1 ¼ lb each), parboiled and meat removed (see pages 17–23)
1 Tbsp Yuzu juice
3 Tbsp sesame oil
1 green apple
1 small bunch chives, finely chopped
1 Tbsp freshly grated ginger
Zest of 1 lemon
¼ cup microgreens (pea shoots or micro basil)

LOBSTER LAGER CHEESE FONDUE

This is a great recipe for fall or winter. It's sure to warm you up, and it's a great way to get into a few beers and talk over some fun food. You don't need much beer for the recipe, so you can drink what you don't cook!

1. Cut the lobster meat into large chunks and place it in a bowl. **2.** In a medium-sized nonstick saucepan, melt the butter over medium heat. Add the shallot and cook until soft. Add the white wine and allow it to reduce by half. **3.** Light the fondue pot burner to begin to heat the pot. **4.** As the fondue pot heats, rub the garlic clove halves around the inside to season it. **5.** In a small saucepan, cook the Swiss cheese, lager, and cornstarch over medium-low heat. Heat until fully melted and mixed. Add the white wine mixture, and stir until heated through. Do not boil. **6.** Pour the cheese mixture into the hot fondue pot. Add the nutmeg and gently stir. **7.** Using the fondue forks, spear lobster chunks, sliced pickles, and cubes of sourdough and dunk into the fondue pot. Easy!

Note: If your cheese mixture is too thick, slowly stir in a little bit of milk until you reach your desired consistency. I use Samuel Adams Boston Lager for this recipe because it adds a nice rich caramel, spicy flavor.

SERVES 4

1 live lobster (about 1 ¼ lb), boiled or steamed and meat removed, or 2 fresh frozen lobster tails, boiled and meat removed (see pages 17–23)

1 Tbsp salted butter

1 shallot, finely diced

½ cup white wine

2 cloves garlic, halved (for seasoning the fondue pot)

½ cup grated Swiss cheese

2 Tbsp lager

1 Tbsp cornstarch

Pinch of freshly grated nutmeg

1 cup sliced pickles, cut no thicker than 1 inch

¼ sourdough loaf, cubed

HOT OIL LOBSTER FONDUE

I've been very blessed to travel to many countries, searching for great food and different cultures. My inspiration for this recipe comes from my travels to Switzerland, where my extended family owns an awesome fondue restaurant.

1. Rinse the lobster meat and cut it into large chunks. **2.** Carefully half-fill a fondue pot with the oil. Light the burner and bring the oil almost to a boil (325°F–350°F). **3.** Use a fondue fork to spear the raw lobster meat and cook it in the hot oil for 1 minute or so, being careful not to burn it. **4.** Dip the fried lobster chunks into your favorite dipping sauce and enjoy!

Note: This recipe uses hot oil to cook the lobster from a fresh, raw state. You can fondue with shrimp, scallops, or vegetables too, if you're into that kind of thing.

SERVES 4

1 live lobster (about 1 ¼ lb) or 2 fresh frozen lobster tails, meat removed (see pages 17–23)
2 cups peanut oil
A small dish of your favorite dip (try Sriracha Mayo, page 191)

OYSTERS ROCK LOBSTAH FELLAH

An old-school dish meets my new-school touch and techniques. Rumor has it that Oysters Rockefeller was created at a New Orleans restaurant and was named after John D. Rockefeller, who was the richest American at the time of its creation.

SERVES 4

1 live lobster (about 1 ¼ lb), boiled and meat removed (see pages 17–23)
12 fresh oysters, washed
1 onion, finely chopped
½ cup salted butter
1 cup finely chopped baby spinach
½ cup grated Parmigiano-Reggiano cheese
1 Tbsp lemon juice
Freshly ground pepper
1 ½ cups Kosher salt (for oyster bed)

1. Finely chop the lobster meat and place it in a bowl. Set aside. **2.** Using an oyster knife, open each oyster, ensuring they are clean and their muscle cord is cut at the bottom of the shell. Put the oyster meat in a bowl, keeping each one intact. Reserve the bottom shells and discard the top shells. **3.** In a large saucepan, sauté the onion in the butter over medium heat until soft. Add the spinach and stir until wilted. Remove from the heat and stir in the lobster meat, cheese, and lemon juice. Season to taste with pepper. **4.** Preheat the oven to 400°F. **5.** Lay an even layer of kosher salt (about 1 Tbsp per oyster) on a rimmed baking sheet. Lightly press the oyster shell bottoms down into the salt to hold them in place. Spoon an oyster into each shell and top with about 2 tsp of the lobster mixture. If there is any remaining mixture, divide it evenly over each oyster shell. Bake, uncovered, for 6 to 8 minutes, or until the cheese has browned. **6.** Serve on a plate or board with a fresh bed of kosher salt (about 1 Tbsp per oyster) to hold the shells in place.

OYSTERS CAESAR-STYLE

Caesars are all the rage in Canada, but I know my friends down south like a Bloody Mary. Take your favorite Caesar or Bloody Mary flavors and pop them into an oyster! This is such an easy way to kick your fresh oysters up a notch. Drink your favorite beer with these.

SERVES 4

1 live lobster (about 1 ¼ lb), boiled and meat removed (see pages 17–23)
1 small Roma tomato, diced
2 oz vodka
2 dashes of hot sauce
Dash of Worcestershire sauce
Juice of 1 lime
Sea salt and freshly ground pepper
½ cup kosher salt (for oyster bed)
12 fresh oysters, washed
¼ cup microgreens (pea shoots or micro basil)

1. Finely chop the lobster meat, place it in a bowl, and put in the refrigerator to cool. **2.** Once the lobster is cool, mix in the tomato, vodka, hot sauce, Worcestershire sauce, lime juice, and salt and pepper to taste. Chill in the refrigerator while you prepare the oysters. **3.** Place the kosher salt on a serving platter or large plate as a bed for the oysters. **4.** Using an oyster knife, open each oyster, ensuring they are clean and their muscle cord is cut at the bottom of the shell. Place them on the kosher salt (discarding the top shells) and evenly top with the Caesar mixture. Garnish with microgreens.

SOUPS AND SALADS

CHILLED SUMMER CORN AND LOBSTER SOUP

Corn soup has been my favorite summer soup for years, especially when made with fresh, sweet local corn. Every summer I look forward to enjoying corn soup made by a guy who has a vendor stall down by the waterfront in Toronto. He's known as the "corn man."

SERVES 4 TO 6

1 live lobster (about 1 ¼ lb),
    boiled and meat removed
    (see pages 17–23)
6 ears fresh corn
¼ cup salted butter
1 shallot, finely chopped
6 cups chicken stock
Kosher salt and freshly
    ground pepper
4 leaves fresh basil,
    finely chopped

1. Chop the lobster meat into small chunks and place it in a bowl, then refrigerate to keep cool until needed. **2.** Clean and wash the corn. Using a knife, scrape the kernels off and break the cobs in half. Set aside. **3.** In a large saucepan, melt the butter over medium-low heat. Add the shallot and cook until soft and translucent. Add the chicken stock, corn kernels, and salt and pepper to taste. Increase the heat to high and bring the mixture to a boil. Once it's boiling, turn down the heat to medium and cook, uncovered, for 8 minutes. **4.** Transfer the soup to a blender or food processor and puree until smooth. Transfer to an airtight container, allow to cool to room temperature, then refrigerate for 30 minutes to 1 hour. **5.** To serve, ladle the cold soup into chilled bowls and top with the lobster meat and fresh basil.

Note: This soup should have a nice creamy consistency without being gloppy. If you find it's too thick, put it in a saucepan and cook over medium heat, adding water or chicken stock (a little bit at a time) until it's thin enough for you.

SAMUEL ADAMS BOSTON LAGER LOBSTAH CHOWDAH

Beer and lobster in a soup bring a smile to my face. Try this amazing and easy recipe for the best chowder you will ever eat. I like to use Samuel Adams Boston Lager for this recipe as it adds rich caramel and hoppy notes to the dish. For some added fun, grab large sourdough bread buns and cut the centers out of them so you can fill them with chowdah!

SERVES 4

1 live lobster (about 1 ¼ lb), boiled and meat removed (see pages 17–23), shells and 10 cups cooking liquid reserved

3 stalks celery, roughly chopped

2 carrots, roughly chopped

1 large white onion, peeled and diced

3 cloves garlic, minced

3 sprigs fresh flat-leaf parsley, roughly chopped

6 black peppercorns

1 bay leaf

6 ears fresh corn

1 bottle (355 ml) lager

1 ½ lb (about 6–8 medium) red potatoes, peeled and cut into ½-inch cubes

3 cups half-and-half cream

1 Tbsp cayenne pepper

Kosher salt and freshly ground pepper

1 bunch chives, finely chopped

1. Roughly chop the lobster meat and place it in a bowl. Set aside. **2.** In the same stockpot you used to cook the lobster, heat the reserved cooking liquid, uncovered, over high heat. Add the lobster shells and bring to a boil. Add the celery, carrots, onion, garlic, parsley, peppercorns, and bay leaf. Turn down the heat to medium-low and simmer, uncovered, for 1 ½ hours, until the soup is creamy and thick. **3.** Using a sharp knife, scrape the kernels off each corn cob into a bowl and set aside. **4.** Strain the lobster broth through a fine mesh sieve into a clean, smaller saucepan. Add the lager and cook, uncovered, over medium-high heat for 10 minutes, or until the broth starts to thicken. Add the potatoes and corn kernels. Turn down the heat to medium and simmer, uncovered, for 10 to 15 minutes, or until the potatoes are tender. Stir in the cream and add the cayenne pepper. Return to a simmer for 10 minutes. Add the lobster meat and continue to simmer, uncovered, for an additional 2 to 4 minutes. Season to taste with salt and pepper. **5.** Ladle the chowder into bowls and top with chopped chives.

Note: Consider using homemade croutons to garnish the soup. Cut your favorite bread into 1-inch cubes, place them directly on a baking sheet, drizzle with olive oil, and season with kosher salt, freshly ground pepper, and dried oregano. Bake at 375°F for 8 to 10 minutes or until golden brown.

LOBSTER CITRUS SALAD

I wish that I had a great story for this dish, but I don't. I am simply a lover of beets who thought of this salad a few summers ago. It's been a real hit since.

SERVES 4 AS A SIDE

4 beets
Kosher salt and freshly
    ground pepper
Extra virgin olive oil
1 live lobster (about 1 ¼ lb),
    boiled and meat removed
    (see pages 17–23)
1 large navel orange
1 large pink grapefruit
Juice of 1 lime
1 Tbsp honey
1 tsp ground cardamom
3 sprigs mint,
    roughly chopped

1. Preheat the oven to 375°F. **2.** Wash and clean the beets. Place them on a large sheet of aluminum foil and sprinkle with a pinch of salt and pepper and a drizzle of olive oil. Roast the beets for 3 hours, or until soft throughout. Once cooked, allow them to cool enough to handle, then peel and slice them into ¼-inch-thick rounds. Set aside to cool completely. **3.** Chop the lobster meat into chunks and place it in a bowl. Set aside in the refrigerator and allow to cool. **4.** Peel the orange and grapefruit. Cut away the white membranes of the individual segments with a sharp knife. **5.** Place the orange and grapefruit segments in a medium-sized mixing bowl with the beets and lobster meat. Add the lime juice, honey, and cardamom. Toss well. **6.** Serve the salad in a cold serving bowl and garnish with mint.

Note: The cardamom gives a nice flavor to the sweet citrus pieces. Did you know that cardamom is third most-expensive spice in the world? It comes in behind vanilla and saffron.

Origin Lobster Salad
Chef Claudio Aprile (Origin)

This recipe was inspired by a trip to Thailand and has become a dish that I feature at my restaurant Origin during the summer seafood season. It absolutely captures the vibrant flavors that Origin has to offer.

1. For the dressing, combine the bird's eye chili in a mixing bowl with the garlic, lime juice, fish sauce, rice vinegar, sesame oil, and cilantro. Set aside in the refrigerator until needed. **2.** Poach the lobster (see page 18). When done, immediately shock the lobster in ice water. Remove the meat from the shell. (The adventurous cook can save the green tamale to incorporate in the Nam Jim Dressing for an intense lobster flavor.) **3.** Slice the cucumber into thin ribbons, using a mandolin. Cook the noodles according to the package directions and allow to cool. **4.** Place the lobster meat, rice noodles, cucumber, and pomelo segments in a mixing bowl and dress lightly with the dressing. Mix well and sprinkle with the sesame seeds. **5.** To serve, put the salad in a wide bowl, ensuring the lobster is toward the top of the pile. Sprinkle with a few more sesame seeds and the crispy fried onions. Finish with the picked cilantro leaves.

SERVES 2 TO 4

Nam Jim Dressing

1 bird's eye (Thai) chili, finely minced
2 cloves garlic, finely minced
¼ cup lime juice
¼ cup fish sauce
¼ cup rice vinegar
¼ cup sesame oil
5–6 sprigs cilantro, finely chopped

Salad

1 live lobster (about 1 ¼ lb)
Maldon sea salt
1 English cucumber
6 oz wide, flat rice noodles
1 pomelo (or 1 small grapefruit + 1 small orange), segmented
1 tsp toasted white sesame seeds
2 Tbsp crispy fried onions (store-bought are fine)
3 sprigs cilantro, picked

THE ROCK'S LBT SALAD

LBT? Lobster – Basil – Tomato. When you combine fresh summer tomatoes with olive oil and fresh basil, life is good. This is an awesome and easy salad to make. Impress your friends by simply adding lobster. You'll look like a champion!

SERVES 4 AS A SIDE

1 live lobster (about 1 ¼ lb), boiled and meat removed (see pages 17–23)
4 tomatoes, chopped
4 fresh basil leaves, roughly chopped
1 Tbsp extra virgin olive oil
Kosher salt and freshly ground pepper

1. Chop the lobster meat into large chunks and place it in a large mixing bowl.
2. Add the tomatoes to the lobster meat with the chopped basil leaves. Drizzle with the extra virgin olive oil and season to taste with salt and pepper.

SEXY ROASTED BEETS AND HEIRLOOM CARROT SALAD

This fun salad has been on my menu since the beginning of Rock Lobster Food Co. The contrast of flavors and colors always makes it a customer favorite. It's great alongside any of the heavier dishes in the Big Plates chapter (pages 109–51).

SERVES 4 AS A SIDE

Salad

6 beets
1 Tbsp olive oil
Kosher salt and freshly
    ground pepper
1 navel orange, cut into
    segments
3 heirloom carrots, peeled
    into long, thin pieces
4 small radishes, thinly sliced
¼ cup crumbled goat cheese
2 pinches of microgreens

Red Wine Vinaigrette

¼ cup red wine vinegar
1 Tbsp olive oil
1 Tbsp maple syrup
Kosher salt and freshly ground
    pepper

1. Preheat the oven to 400°F. **2.** In a bowl, toss the beets in the 1 Tbsp olive oil, season to taste with salt and pepper, and wrap in aluminum foil. Bake for 2 hours, or until soft. Remove the beets from the oven and peel while hot. Cut each beet into quarters. Set aside to cool. **3.** For the dressing, combine the red wine vinegar, olive oil, and maple syrup in a large bowl and stir well. Season to taste with salt and pepper. **4.** Add the oranges, carrots, and beets to the dressing. Gently toss to coat. Transfer to a serving plate, place the radishes on top, sprinkle with goat cheese, and garnish with microgreens.

Note: The dressing for this salad can be refrigerated in an airtight container for up to 1 month. If you want the carrot strips to curl and be crispy, place them in ice-cold water for a minimum of 1 hour prior to making the salad.

SUMMER WATERMELON FETA SALAD

SERVES 4 AS A SIDE

⅓ cup balsamic vinegar
¼ cup olive oil
Kosher salt and freshly ground
  pepper
1 medium watermelon, rind
  removed
¼ cup diced black olives
1 cup crumbled Greek feta
  cheese
1 bunch fresh mint, finely
  chopped

This salad's crisp sweetness is a great balance for any of the rich, creamy dishes in the Big Plates chapter (pages 109–51). You can also try grilling the watermelon on the BBQ if you fancy a change. The heat and smoky flavor transform the salad.

1. In a small mixing bowl, whisk together the balsamic vinegar and olive oil. Season to taste with salt and pepper. **2.** Cut the watermelon into rectangles, 1 inch long. **3.** On each serving plate, lay out three pieces of watermelon and spoon the black olives on top. Top with the crumbled feta cheese and drizzle with the balsamic dressing. Garnish with a little bit of mint for an extra hint of flavor.

Note: The easiest way to cut mint leaves is to stack them and roll them into a cigar shape before slicing. Slice them thinly for chiffonade mint leaves.

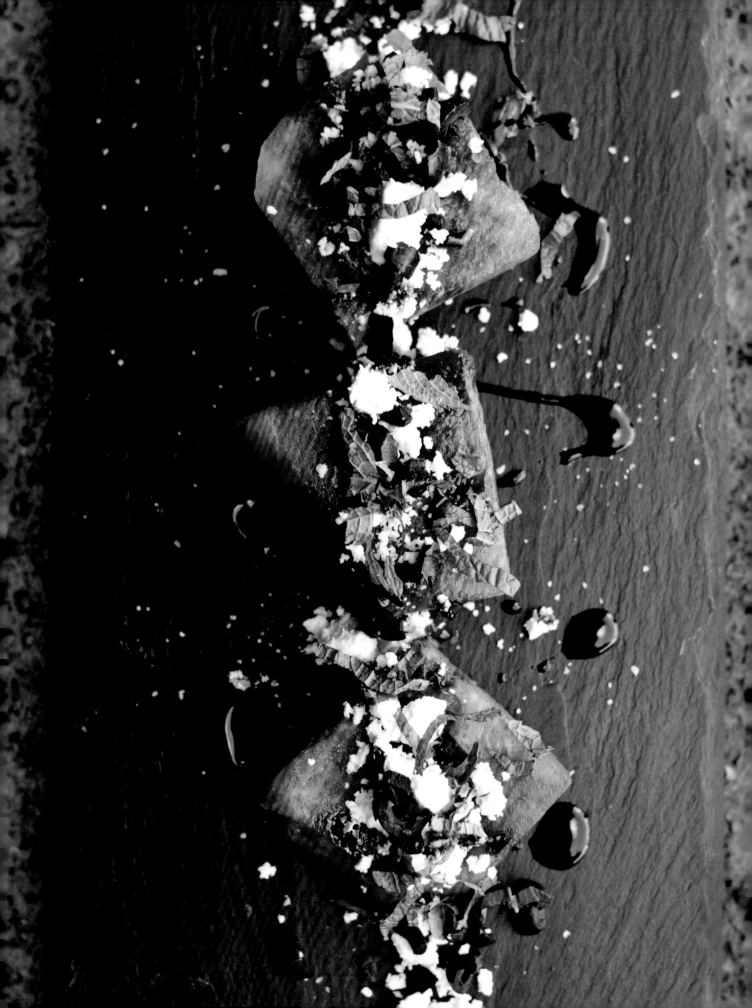

ROLLS,
TACOS,
AND BURGERS

MAINE HOT LOBSTER ROLL

There are many different kinds of lobster rolls. The two best, in my humble opinion, are

1. Served hot with large chunks of lobster and hot drawn butter poured overtop.
2. Served cold with chopped lobster, mayonnaise, seasoning, and lemon juice.

This recipe is for #1, the hot roll. You'll find #2, the cold roll, my famous Rock Lobster Roll, on page 101. Try them both and see which one you prefer.

SERVES 4

1 live lobster (about 1 ¼ lb), boiled and meat removed (see pages 17–23)
Juice of 1 lemon
1 tsp Old Bay Seasoning (or your favorite seafood seasoning)
3 Tbsp salted butter
4 top-loader or top-sliced hot dog buns
Chips for serving

1. Roughly chop the lobster meat and place it in a bowl. Add the lemon juice and seafood seasoning. Toss well to coat the lobster meat. **2.** In a small saucepan, melt 2 Tbsp of the butter over medium heat. Keep it warm. **3.** Butter the buns using the remaining 1 Tbsp of the butter. Place the buns on a hot grill top or in a frying pan and toast each side until golden brown or to your liking. **4.** Evenly spoon the lobster mixture into the toasted buns and pour hot butter on top of the lobster. Serve immediately with your favorite chips.

Note: The key to the perfect lobster roll is using a "top-loader" or "top-sliced" bun rather than a brioche or thick, bready hot dog bun. You can make your own by simply cutting some excess bread off both sides of a regular hot dog bun.

ROCK LOBSTER ROLL

This right here is how it all started. In early 2012, I set myself a goal to make lobster more accessible to Canadians, and the lobster roll was my way of doing just that. We started selling our lobster rolls from a table at a pop-up event and now they have their own cult following. This recipe is near and dear to my heart. I hope you enjoy making them as much as we do!

SERVES 4

1 live lobster (about 1 ¼ lb), boiled and meat removed (see pages 17–23)
¼ cup mayonnaise
Juice of ½ lemon
1 Tbsp Old Bay Seasoning (or your favorite seafood seasoning)
Kosher salt and freshly ground pepper
4 top-sliced hot dog buns (see Note)
1 Tbsp unsalted butter
2 pickles, sliced in half lengthwise
Chips for serving

1. Coarsely chop the lobster meat and place it in a mixing bowl. Add the mayonnaise, lemon juice, seafood seasoning, and a pinch of salt and pepper. Mix gently. **2.** Butter each side of the buns. On a grill top over medium heat or in a frying pan, toast them on each side. **3.** Evenly spoon the lobster mixture into the toasted buns. Serve with pickles and chips on the side.

Note: This recipe is great accompanied by chips and pickles. In our restaurants, we use McClure's pickles. I highly recommend them! The lobster mixture can be refrigerated for up to 2 days.

RLFC LOBSTER MELT

This is roadside diner meets Las Vegas. I say Vegas because everything is big and bold! Just like this sandwich. With this recipe, I take an all-time diner favorite and kick it up a notch with an elegant cheese and the King of the Sea. Once you try it, you'll never reach for canned tuna again.

SERVES 4

2 fresh frozen lobster tails, steamed and meat removed (see pages 21–23)
1 stalk celery, finely diced
1 Tbsp mayonnaise
1 tsp Old Bay Seasoning (or your favorite seafood seasoning)
1 sprig fresh dill, diced
8 slices quality sourdough bread
8 small slices Brie cheese, rind on

1. Preheat the broiler to high heat. **2.** Cut the lobster meat into medallions and place it in a mixing bowl. **3.** Add the celery, mayonnaise, seafood seasoning, and dill to the lobster. Mix well, keeping the medallion shapes intact. **4.** Spoon some of the lobster mixture onto a slice of bread. Top with a slice of Brie and cover with a slice of bread. Repeat with the remaining ingredients to make four sandwiches in total. **5.** Broil the sandwiches for 3 to 5 minutes, flipping once, or until the cheese is melted. Serve immediately.

TEQUILA LIME LOBSTER TAQUITOS WITH SPICY SOUR CREAM

SERVES 4

Spicy Sour Cream
 (see page 190)
Vegetable oil
2 live lobsters (about 1 ¼ lb
 each), parboiled and meat
 removed (see pages 17–23)
1 ½ tsp smoked paprika
1 ½ tsp chili powder
1 ½ tsp dry mustard
1 large white onion, diced
1 clove garlic, minced
3 Tbsp finely chopped cilantro
2 oz quality tequila
1 cup shredded aged
 Cheddar cheese
3 limes
12 corn tortillas

Street food is becoming extremely popular, and I absolutely love it. Here is my take on this classic Latino street food that's made around the globe.

1. Prepare the Spicy Sour Cream. **2.** Preheat the oven to 375°F. Lightly grease a baking sheet with vegetable oil. **3.** Finely chop the lobster meat and place it in a bowl. Set aside. **4.** In a large bowl, combine the smoked paprika, chili powder, and dry mustard with the onion, garlic, and 1 Tbsp of the cilantro. Add the lobster meat, tequila, cheese, and the juice of 1 lime. Mix well. Set aside. **5.** In a hot frying pan, warm each tortilla for 10 to 15 seconds over high heat. This will help soften them and make them easier to fold. **6.** Evenly spoon the lobster mixture into the center of each tortilla and roll up tightly. Place the wrapped tortillas on the greased baking sheet, seam side down, and drizzle them with vegetable oil. Bake for 12 to 15 minutes, or until the insides are heated through and the outsides are golden brown. **7.** Quarter the remaining 2 limes. Place three taquitos per person on a plate. Drizzle with the sour cream and garnish with the remaining 2 Tbsp of the cilantro and limes. Serve immediately.

Note: This recipe bakes the taquitos, but feel free to deep-fry them for some added crunch. I like to use only premium tequila. One of my personal favorites is Tromba (100% pure agave), a brand created by one of my closest friends, Eric Brass.

DC'S BBQ LOBSTER BURGER

This burger idea and recipe came from a dear friend of mine, Danny Cameron!

1. Cut the whole lobster meat into ¼-inch-thick medallions and place it in a bowl. Set aside. **2.** Preheat the grill to medium (around 350°F). **3.** In a large mixing bowl, combine the ground beef with the egg, breadcrumbs, lemon juice, thyme, rosemary, and salt and pepper to taste. Shape the meat mixture into patties, about 3 inches in diameter and 1 inch thick. **4.** Grill the burgers for 4 to 5 minutes per side for medium-well doneness. **5.** Grill the buns for 1 minute, or toast to your liking. **6.** Spread the toasted bun bottoms with mayonnaise, top each with a lettuce leaf, add a burger, and top with a medallion of lobster meat. Sprinkle with chopped chives and complete with the bun top. Serve with kettle potato chips on the side.

SERVES 4

2 live lobsters (about 1 ¼ lb), boiled and meat removed, or 2 fresh frozen lobster tails, boiled and meat removed (see pages 17–23)
1 lb medium ground beef
1 egg
½ cup dried Italian breadcrumbs
Juice of 1 lemon
1 Tbsp chopped fresh thyme
1 Tbsp finely chopped fresh rosemary
Kosher salt and freshly ground pepper
4 sesame seed hamburger buns
3 Tbsp mayonnaise
4 leaves Bibb lettuce
1 bunch chives, finely chopped
Kettle potato chips for serving

BIG PLATES

CLASSIC LOBSTER BOIL

This still has to be one of my favorite ways to eat a lobster. Nothing is more fun than sitting at the dock, in the park, or at your family's table with everyone dipping warm, succulent lobster into hot drawn butter. Holy smokes, now I'm hungry! I hope you are too! If you're doing this boil in the summer months, make sure to grab some sweet, local corn and throw it into the saucepan as well.

SERVES 4

1 Tbsp kosher salt
2 white onions,
    roughly chopped
2 lemons, halved
1 orange, halved
1 head celery,
    roughly chopped
4 live lobsters
    (about 1 ¼ lb each)
    4 ears corn
½ cup Clarified Butter
    (page 189)

1. Fill a large stockpot with water, add the kosher salt, and bring to a boil. Add the onions, lemon halves, orange halves, and celery. Bring to a full rolling boil for 15 minutes to allow the flavors to develop. Add the live lobsters and boil for 8 minutes. Add the corn (or you can cook the corn in a separate saucepan if you're running short of space) and boil for an additional 4 to 5 minutes. **2.** In a separate small saucepan, melt the butter over medium heat. **3.** Place a corn cob and a lobster on each of four plates, crack the shell, dip the meat in butter, and enjoy!

BUTTERFLIED LOBSTER TAILS WITH GARLIC-LEMON BUTTER

If you want to impress your friends, simply learn this easy-to-do recipe for your next dinner party. I love to pair these lobster tails with creamed spinach, hot bread rolls, melted butter, and lots of vino!

SERVES 4

4 fresh frozen lobster tails
⅓ cup salted butter
1 head garlic, minced
1 small bunch chives,
    finely chopped
Juice of 1 lemon

1. Thaw the lobster tails. Rinse and pat dry with paper towel. **2.** To butterfly the tails, use kitchen shears or a sharp knife to cut lengthwise through the center of the hard top shells and meat, cutting down to but not through the bottom of the shells. Prise the shell halves apart with your fingers and pull the meat upward, setting it on the back of the cut shells. **3.** In a small saucepan, melt the butter over medium heat and add the garlic. Remove the pan from the heat. Stir in the chives and lemon juice. Remove 2 Tbsp of this sauce and reserve it in a small bowl. Place the remaining sauce in a separate small bowl. **4.** Preheat the grill to medium heat (around 350°F). **5.** Brush the lobster meat with the 2 Tbsp of the reserved butter sauce. **6.** Place the lobster tails on the grill, meat side down. Close the lid and grill for 4 to 5 minutes. Remove the lobster tails from the grill and brush with the remaining butter sauce before serving.

CAMPFIRE-SMOKED LOBSTER TAILS WRAPPED IN FOIL

This is the ultimate recipe when you are camping or at the cottage. Start a fire, wrap your lobster tails, and you're all set! I recommend serving this with a great macaroni or potato salad and buttered corn for a perfect campfire meal.

SERVES 4

4 fresh frozen lobster tails, thawed
2 lemons, sliced into rounds
½ cup salted butter, sliced
4 sprigs fresh dill

1. Prepare a campfire, ensuring that the coals are nice and hot. **2.** Place the thawed lobster tails, lemon slices, butter slices, and dill on a large sheet of aluminum foil. Wrap and seal the foil around the lobster tails to create a pouch. **3.** Place the foil pouch, seam side up, on the hot coals (the foil pouch should not be in direct contact with flames) and cook for 10 minutes, or until the meat is firm and white. Be sure to use tongs to open the pouch, taking care not to scald yourself with the steam.

Note: Cooking the lobster tails in an aluminum foil pouch gives the seafood a smoky taste. Add a few cherry wood chips to the foil pouch to add some serious flavor.

PANCETTA-WRAPPED LOBSTER TAILS WITH LEMON-PARSLEY SAUCE

SERVES 4

2 fresh frozen lobster tails, thawed
2 cloves garlic, minced
¼ cup extra virgin olive oil (plus extra for brushing)
Zest of 1 lemon
¼ cup lemon juice
¼ cup roughly chopped fresh flat-leaf parsley
¼ tsp cayenne pepper
4 pieces thinly sliced pancetta

There is only one way to make lobster better and that is to wrap it in bacon! I like to use pancetta as it's thin and salty. These are great served with Matty's Seafood Sauce (page 186) on the side.

1. Preheat the oven to 375°F. **2.** Carefully remove the tail meat from the thawed lobster tails and place it in a bowl. Set aside. **3.** In a medium-sized bowl, combine the garlic, olive oil, lemon zest and juice, parsley, and cayenne pepper. Gently mix to combine. **4.** Roll the uncooked lobster tail meat in the marinade to thoroughly coat it. Wrap each lobster tail in two pancetta slices. Brush the wrapped tails with a little bit of olive oil to prevent burning. **5.** Lightly oil a baking sheet. **6.** In a large nonstick frying pan, sear the wrapped lobster tails for 1 to 2 minutes per side over medium-high heat to brown and lock in the flavors. Transfer to the prepared baking sheet and bake in the oven for 5 to 6 minutes, or until the tails are firm and opaque and the pancetta is crisp. Serve immediately.

BANG'N COCONUT CURRY LOBSTER TAILS

Every time I make this dish I think of Southeast Asia and how much I want to go there. It's a region full of flavors—spices, herbs, chilis, wet and dry curries—and I'm planning a culinary trip there sometime soon. I know that I'm going to come back inspired by the experience.

SERVES 4

4 fresh frozen lobster tails, steamed (see pages 21–23)
2 Tbsp peanut oil
2 cloves garlic, minced
3 tsp red curry paste
1 small Spanish onion, finely chopped
1 yellow bell pepper, cut into thin strips
1 can (14 oz) unsweetened coconut milk
¾ cup heavy cream
½ cinnamon stick
½ tsp coriander seeds
¼ tsp ground turmeric
½ tsp fish sauce
1 tomato, finely chopped
½ cup finely chopped cilantro

1. Cut the steamed lobster tails in half using a large chef's knife, leaving the meat in the shells. Set aside. **2.** In a large frying pan, warm the oil over medium heat. Add the garlic and curry paste and sauté for 1 minute. Add the onion and bell pepper and sauté for 2 minutes. Increase the temperature to high, add the coconut milk, and simmer for 15 to 20 minutes, until the mixture reduces by half. Do not allow the mixture to boil. **3.** Stir in the cream and simmer for 2 to 3 minutes, or until the sauce reduces and thickens. Add the cinnamon stick, coriander seeds, turmeric, fish sauce, tomato, and lobster tails (still in their shells). Cook for 1 to 2 minutes, stirring well. **4.** Serve in bowls, garnished with cilantro. You can also serve this on a bed of jasmine rice.

Note: You can crank up the heat by adding long, thin green finger chilis.

LOBSTER AND TENDERLOIN SKEWERS

The King of the Sea meets the King of the Land! These skewers are fun to make and eat. Make these for your next dinner party to give your guests the best of both worlds. I recommend pairing these skewers with loaded baked potatoes—add some bacon, sour cream, shredded cheddar cheese, and green onions and you're off to a great meal.

SERVES 4

2 fresh frozen lobster tails, parboiled and meat removed (see pages 21–23)
2 Tbsp extra virgin olive oil
1 Tbsp red wine vinegar
Juice of 1 lemon
2 Tbsp finely chopped fresh thyme
Kosher salt and freshly ground pepper
8 oz beef tenderloin
1 yellow bell pepper, roughly chopped
1 ½ tsp smoked paprika
Vegetable or canola oil

1. If you're using wooden skewers, place them in cold water to soak for at least 1 hour before you plan to serve dinner. **2.** Cut the lobster tail meat pieces into large cubes and place it in a bowl. Set aside. **3.** In a large mixing bowl, combine the olive oil and red wine vinegar with the lemon juice and thyme. Season to taste with salt and pepper and whisk together. Set aside. **4.** Cut the beef tenderloin into large cubes, roughly the same size as the lobster meat, and place it in the marinade. Add the lobster meat, cover, and refrigerate for a minimum of 2 hours to marinate. **5.** Preheat the grill to medium heat (around 350°F). **6.** Spike a piece of beef on a skewer, followed by a cube of lobster meat, and then a piece of bell pepper. Continue in this way until the skewer is full, then sprinkle with smoked paprika. Repeat with the remaining skewers until all the meat has been used. **7.** While the grill is warming, season the grate with a little bit of oil to ensure that the meat does not stick. **8.** Grill the skewers for 3 minutes on each side or until fully cooked. Watch carefully to ensure they don't burn. Serve immediately.

Note: If you want to make these often, I suggest you buy metal skewers. Not only will you always have skewers on hand, you will also be able to skip the wooden skewer soaking stage.

LOBSTER-STUFFED FLANK STEAK PINWHEELS

This recipe came about from my love of surf and turf. When I started making this dish, I found that it was easy to accidentally overcook both meats, so take care to keep a close eye on them. Try pairing this dish with delicious steamed asparagus topped with Parmesan cheese shavings.

SERVES 4

1 live lobster (about 1 ¼ lb), parboiled and meat removed (see pages 17–23)
1 Tbsp grated lemon zest
1 lb flank steak
Kosher salt and freshly ground pepper
¼ cup extra virgin olive oil

1. Place the lobster meat on a cutting board and cover with a piece of plastic wrap. Using a kitchen mallet, flatten the meat so that it's 3 inches x 6 inches and ¼ inch thick, and then sprinkle with the lemon zest. **2.** Place the flank steak on a separate cutting board and cover it with a piece of plastic wrap. Using a kitchen mallet, flatten the meat so that it's also 3 inches x 6 inches and ¼ inch thick. Season to taste with salt and pepper. **3.** On a flat work surface, lay out the flank steak and top it with the flattened lobster meat. Roll up tightly, with the lobster as the inside layer, and secure with metal skewers, about 1 inch apart. **4.** Move the oven rack to the highest level in the oven and set the broiler to high. **5.** Grease a rimmed baking sheet with the olive oil and place the skewered roll on it. Broil the roll for 4 to 5 minutes, then turn it over and broil for an additional 4 to 5 minutes. Remove from the oven immediately. Watch it carefully so you don't burn it. **6.** Slice the rolled flank steak in between the skewers to create pinwheels. Remove the skewers from the pinwheels and garnish with salt to taste.

DIGBY SCALLOPS WITH LOBSTER BUTTER

SERVES 4

2 Tbsp Lobster Butter (page 190)
12 fresh Digby (sea) scallops
Kosher salt and freshly ground pepper
1 lemon
1 small bunch chives, finely chopped
¼ cup microgreens (pea shoots or micro basil)

This dish is a quick and simple meal. Lobster Mashed Potatoes (page 160) are the perfect accompaniment. I love to use fresh Digby scallops. In my opinion, they are some of the best in the world. Nova Scotia even has an amazing annual Digby scallop festival that I strongly suggest you check out!

1. Prepare the Lobster Butter. **2.** Pat the scallops dry with paper towel and season to taste with salt and pepper. **3.** Preheat the oven to 375°F and warm a plate in the oven for a couple of minutes while the scallops are searing. **4.** In a large frying pan, warm 1 Tbsp of the lobster butter over medium-high heat. When the pan is very hot and the butter has melted, add the scallops. Sear the scallops until golden brown on one side, without moving, about 2 minutes, then flip and cook on the other side for 1 minute or until golden brown. You're looking for an even sear on both sides to lock in the flavor. Add the remaining 1 Tbsp of the lobster butter to the scallops in the frying pan and let it melt. Remove the scallops from the pan and rest them briefly on the warm plate. **5.** Transfer to a serving plate and top with the lobster butter from the pan. Garnish with a squeeze of lemon juice, a sprinkling of chives and some microgreens with lemon wedges on the side.

Note: I suggest using U-10 (under 10 pieces per pound) sized scallops, as these work best for searing medium to medium-rare. Make sure that your scallops are dry before searing them as they won't sear properly if waterlogged. Did you know that scallops are 80% water? You do now!

SMOKED BACON–WRAPPED LOBSTER AND SCALLOPS

My mom has been making bacon-wrapped scallops since I was about four years old. She taught me how to make this dish, minus the lobster (I added that years later), before I went to university. Talk about the ultimate dorm room meal.

SERVES 4

1 live lobster (about 1 ½ lb),
    parboiled and meat removed
    (see pages 17–23)
12 fresh large scallops
Kosher salt and freshly
    ground pepper
12 slices smoked bacon
1 cup white wine
Juice of 1 lemon
2 sprigs rosemary, finely
    chopped
¼ cup salted butter

1. Cut the lobster meat into 12 evenly sized cubes and place it in a bowl. Set aside. **2.** Preheat the oven to 375°F. Lightly grease a baking sheet. **3.** Dry the scallops thoroughly with paper towel and season to taste with salt and pepper. Top each scallop with a cube of lobster meat. **4.** Lay out the bacon on a large cutting board. Place a scallop at the bottom of a bacon slice and tightly roll up the bacon to encase the scallop and lobster chunk. Stick a small toothpick in the top side to hold it all together. Place the wrapped scallop on the baking sheet. Repeat with the remaining scallops, lobster, and bacon. **5.** Cover the scallops with foil, so they don't burn. Place the scallops in the oven and bake for 15 to 20 minutes, or until the bacon is brown and crispy. **6.** While the scallops are cooking, combine the white wine, lemon juice, and rosemary in a saucepan and warm over medium heat. Increase the temperature to high and bring to a boil. Turn down the heat to medium and simmer for 8 to 10 minutes, or until the liquid has reduced by half. Add the butter and stir well until melted. Set aside. **7.** Place three cooked scallops on each of four plates and spoon over the white wine sauce. Serve immediately.

Note: Dip these babies in Matty's Seafood Sauce (page 186) for some zip.

THE HAPPY SAILOR LOBSTER AND SCALLOP THERMIDOR

Lobster thermidor was originally a French dish, created in Paris in the late 1800s. I had it for the first time a few years ago and simply fell in love with it. The traditional French recipe calls for brandy or cognac, but I think it tastes best with Sailor Jerry rum.

SERVES 4

2 live lobsters (about 1 ¼ lb each), parboiled and meat removed (see pages 17–23), shells reserved
4 fresh large scallops
2 Tbsp salted butter
1 clove garlic, finely diced
1 shallot, finely diced
2 oz spiced rum
1 cup heavy cream
2 egg yolks
1 Tbsp Dijon mustard
2 Tbsp dried Italian bread-crumbs
½ cup shredded Gruyère cheese
2 Tbsp fresh flat-leaf parsley, finely chopped
1 lemon, quartered

1. Cut the lobster meat into bite-sized pieces and place it in a bowl. **2.** Dry the scallops with paper towel, then cut each one in half horizontally. **3.** In a medium-sized saucepan, melt the butter over medium heat. Add the garlic and shallot and sauté until the shallot is translucent. Turn down the heat to medium-low, add the rum, and simmer for 2 to 3 minutes, or until almost completely reduced. **4.** Meanwhile, in a separate small saucepan, warm the cream over medium heat. Add the heated cream to the reduced shallot-rum mixture. Turn down the heat to low and whisk in the egg yolks. Continue to whisk until this custard has thickened. Add the lobster meat, scallops, and mustard and cook for 2 minutes, or until heated through. **5.** Preheat the oven's broiler to high. **6.** On a large baking sheet, lay out the lobster shells and spoon the hot custard mixture into the body and tail sections. Sprinkle with the breadcrumbs and top with the cheese. Set under the broiler and broil until the cheese is golden brown and bubbling. Remove from the heat and allow to cool slightly. **7.** Serve the broiled lobster on a platter, garnished with parsley and lemon wedges.

Note: When cooking with alcohol, keep a lid handy to put out any flames that don't go out by themselves after 30 seconds or so.

RAGIN' CREOLE SPICY LOBSTER AND SHRIMP

Seafood is a staple in New Orleans and always has been, because the city is so close to the Gulf of Mexico. Some of the treasures you'll find in cooking there include large shrimp, crawfish, and beautiful oysters! After an amazing trip to the Big Easy, I was inspired to make this Creole dish. What a food town it is! A must-visit, if you ask me.

1. Using a large knife, cut the cooked lobster tails in half, leaving the shell on. Set aside. **2.** In a large saucepan, heat the olive oil over medium heat. Add the onion, garlic, and bell pepper and sauté until soft. **3.** Stir in the tomatoes, tomato paste, bourbon, and vinegar. Bring the mixture to a steady simmer, stirring constantly, and cook for 4 to 6 minutes, or until heated through and mixed well. Season to taste with salt and pepper. **4.** Add the cooked lobster (still in the shell) and shrimp and simmer, uncovered, for 6 to 8 minutes, or until the shrimp are cooked through. **5.** Serve in bowls, garnished with parsley and a dash of hot sauce.

Note: I like to serve this with white rice and a big loaf of bread to soak up the sauce.

SERVES 4

4 fresh frozen lobster tails, boiled (see page 21)
2 Tbsp extra virgin olive oil
1 Spanish onion, finely diced
4 cloves garlic, minced
1 red bell pepper, diced
2 large tomatoes, seeded and finely chopped
1 can (6 oz) tomato paste
¼ cup bourbon
1 tsp white vinegar
Kosher salt and freshly ground pepper
1 lb frozen large shrimps, thawed, shells removed
2 sprigs fresh flat-leaf parsley, finely chopped
Hot sauce

Spicy Coconut and Red Pepper Lobster

Chef Roger Mooking

(formerly of Kultura and Nyood)

SERVES 4

Lobster

1 Tbsp coconut or
   grapeseed oil
1 cup chopped leek,
   white parts only
3 cloves garlic
2 Tbsp coriander seeds
1 tsp fennel seeds
Sea salt
4 whole lobsters (1 ½ lb each)

Spicy Coconut Red Pepper Sauce

1 cup roasted red pepper
   puree (store-bought)
¾ cup coconut milk
1 Tbsp soy sauce
½ Tbsp red wine vinegar
2 bird's eye (Thai) chilis,
   thinly sliced
½ tsp dark coconut or
   brown sugar
½ tsp ground cumin
1 Tbsp lemon juice
Freshly ground black pepper

To Finish

2 Tbsp coconut or
   vegetable oil
⅓ cup finely diced shallots
   (about 4 shallots)
½ cup finely chopped
   cilantro or chives

When Matty asked me to contribute a recipe to this book, I wanted to make sure it was simple enough that you, the reader, would actually want to try it. Most important though, the dish had to have a walloping flavor profile that still allowed the main ingredients' natural magic to shine through. The various simple cooking methods used come from growing up watching the chefs in my dad's Chinese restaurant as they manned the woks. Mixed with a little of the French culinary training techniques I've learned over the years, this recipe captures the spirit of my style of cooking: globally inspired and flavor packed. Food is love. Spread the love.

1. Place the coconut oil, then the leek, garlic, coriander seeds, and fennel seeds in a large pot. Sweat over medium heat, without browning, then add enough water to fully submerge the lobsters and bring to a boil. Season the water with sea salt until it tastes like seawater. **2.** Turn down to a simmer and add the lobsters. Cook, uncovered, for 4 minutes, then remove the pot from the heat and allow the lobsters to rest in the hot water for another minute. Remove the lobsters from the pot and place them on a baking sheet in a single layer to cool completely. **3.** Discard the remaining contents of the pot. **4.** For the sauce, place the red pepper puree, coconut milk, soy sauce, red wine vinegar, chilis, sugar, and cumin in a separate saucepan. Bring to a simmer and cook, uncovered, for 25 minutes over medium-low heat. Finish by drizzling with the lemon juice and seasoning to taste with pepper.
5. Once the lobsters are cool, remove the tails and legs (including claws) from the body of the lobster by twisting them. Using a sharp chef's knife, slit each tail in half lengthwise. Hold the claws firmly at one end and crack them so they will be easy to eat. Discard the body of the lobster or use for lobster stock (see page 186).
6. To finish, heat a large frying pan over high heat and add the coconut oil, then the lobster tails and claws. Cook for another 2 minutes or until just heated through. Add the shallots and sauté for about 30 seconds or until the shallots begin to color. Add the sauce and gently mix everything together in the pan until heated through and fully cooked. **7.** Transfer to a serving plate and garnish with cilantro or chives. Serve hot with chunks of oiled and grilled sourdough baguette.

ISLAND-STYLE JERK LOBSTER, SHRIMP AND CRAB

SERVES 2

2 fresh frozen lobster tails,
    boiled (see page 21)
2 clusters (about 1 lb in total)
    frozen Atlantic snow crab
    (see Note)
8 medium-sized fresh shrimp
1 Tbsp unsalted butter
¼ cup jerk seasoning
¼ cup cilantro
1 lime, quartered

This recipe's inspiration came from a few trips to Jamaica. I love Jamaica's spicy food, ice-cold beers, and warm island hospitality. While on vacation there, I get up early, relax on the beach, and then hit up the grill for some jerk chicken—and, if I'm lucky enough, some lobster!

1. Using a large knife, cut the lobster tails in half, leaving the shell on. **2.** Bring a medium-sized saucepan of salted water to a boil. Submerge the crab clusters and cook for 3 to 4 minutes, until heated through. **3.** Remove the crab from the saucepan and use a large knife to cut a slit down the back center of each crab—you are aiming to puncture the shell with one good, long score, to allow the seasoning to set into the meat in the next step. **4.** In a large frying pan, melt the butter over medium heat. Add the jerk seasoning and stir to combine. Add the lobster tails, shrimp and snow crab clusters and sauté for 2 to 3 minutes, or until heated through. **5.** Place the lobster tails and snow crab clusters in a large bowl and drizzle with the seasoned butter. Garnish with cilantro and serve with lime quarters on the side for squeezing.

`Note:` A crab cluster means one whole crab with its center, knuckles, and legs (this recipe calls for two).

SPICY LOBSTER AND SHRIMP MANGO SKEWERS

Savory, smoky, and sweet on a stick. Delicious! Pair this great dish with some basmati rice or coconut milk rice.

SERVES 4

1 live lobster (about 1 ¼ lb),
    parboiled and meat removed
    (see pages 17–23)
4 cloves garlic, minced
1 cup orange juice
2 tsp ground cumin
1 tsp smoked paprika
Cayenne pepper
Kosher salt and freshly
    ground pepper
1 ½ lb large shrimp,
    peeled, deveined, and
    tails removed
1 large mango, peeled and
    cut into cubes
2 limes
¼ cup crushed salted peanuts

1. If you're using wooden skewers, place them in cold water to soak for at least 1 hour before you grill. **2.** Cut the lobster meat into bite-sized cubes and place them in a bowl. Set aside. **3.** In a separate large bowl, mix the garlic with the orange juice, cumin, paprika, and a pinch of cayenne pepper, salt, and pepper. Add half of the lobster meat and all of the shrimp. Set aside and allow to marinate for 30 minutes. **4.** Thread the lobster meat, mango, and shrimp onto the skewers. Continue until all the skewers are full. **5.** Preheat the grill to medium-high heat (350°F–375°F). **6.** Place the skewers on the grill and cook for 2 to 3 minutes on each side. Place the grilled skewers on a serving platter, add a squeeze of lime juice, and sprinkle with crushed peanuts. Serve immediately.

LATE-NIGHT KOREAN SPICY BEEF AND LOBSTER

This dish reminds me of great late-night Korean BBQ in amazing low-key restaurants. Try this foolproof dish at home, and pair it with Thai glass, vermicelli, or soba noodles.

SERVES 4

1 live lobster (about 1 ¼ lb),
    steamed and meat removed
    (see pages 17–23)
1 lb beef tenderloin
2 cloves garlic, minced
1 Tbsp freshly grated ginger
1 Tbsp brown sugar
2 Tbsp soy sauce
1 Tbsp Sriracha sauce
1 Tbsp sesame oil
4 green onions,
    finely chopped

1. Roughly chop the lobster meat and place it in a bowl. Set aside. **2.** Thinly slice the beef tenderloin. **3.** In a large bowl, mix the garlic, ginger, and brown sugar with the soy and Sriracha sauces and 3 Tbsp of water. Add the beef tenderloin slices to this marinade. Cover and refrigerate for 30 minutes to 1 hour to marinate. **4.** In a large frying pan, heat the sesame oil over medium-high heat. Add the marinated beef and the lobster meat. Cook for 2 to 3 minutes, or until completely heated through. **5.** Place the beef and lobster meat on a large serving plate and garnish with green onion.

Note: Place the beef tenderloin in the freezer for 30 minutes to 1 hour prior to cooking as this makes it easier to thinly slice. Always cut the tenderloin against the grain of the meat.

"CAN'T BELIEVE IT'S NOT TAKEOUT" LOBSTER FRIED RICE

Put the phone down! Stop calling your local Chinese restaurant for delivery, and make this quick and easy fried rice at home instead.

SERVES 4

2 cups long-grain rice
1 live lobster (about 1 ¼ lb), boiled and meat removed (see pages 17–23)
2 Tbsp sesame oil (for frying)
1 Tbsp salted butter
1 clove garlic, minced
1 cup frozen mixed vegetables (peas, carrots, corn), thawed
2 eggs, beaten
3 green onions, finely chopped
1 Tbsp soy sauce

1. In a medium-sized saucepan, combine 3 ½ cups of water with the long-grain rice. Bring to a boil and cook, uncovered, for about 8 minutes. Cover the saucepan, turn down the heat to low, and continue to cook for 10 minutes, or until the rice has absorbed most of the water. Remove from the heat and let it rest, covered, for 5 minutes. Then use a fork to fluff the rice to prevent it from clumping. **2.** Cut the lobster meat into bite-sized pieces and place it in a bowl. Set aside. **3.** In a wok or large nonstick frying pan, heat the sesame oil over medium-high heat. Add the butter, then the garlic and vegetables. Cook the vegetables until tender. **4.** Turn down the heat to medium, add the beaten eggs, and stir well into the vegetables. Add the warm cooked rice, lobster meat, and green onions. Mix well. Add the soy sauce and stir until heated through. Serve immediately.

Note: Add 1 Tbsp of butter to the warm cooked rice for a rich, creamy flavor.

STIR-FRIED LOBSTER

I love a good stir-fry. One of the first meals that I can remember my mother teaching me was a stir-fry. By the age of 13, learning how to cook with oyster sauce was my new favorite pastime! You can serve noodles or rice on the side with this, but it's equally good on its own.

SERVES 4

2 live lobsters (about 1 ¼ lb each), boiled and meat removed, or 4 fresh frozen lobster tails, boiled and meat removed (see pages 17–23)
1 tsp cornstarch
2 Tbsp peanut oil
4 green onions, finely chopped
2 Tbsp hoisin sauce
1 tsp Sriracha sauce
30 green beans, ends snipped
¼ cup sliced almonds
2 cloves garlic, minced
1 tsp freshly grated ginger

1. Cut the lobster meat into large pieces. Place in a bowl, sprinkle with the cornstarch, and toss to coat evenly. This will help to seal the meat and keep it tender. **2.** In a wok or large nonstick frying pan, warm the peanut oil over medium heat. Add the green onions and lobster meat. Cook for 5 minutes, stirring occasionally. Add the hoisin and Sriracha sauces, then the green beans, almonds, garlic, ginger, and 1 Tbsp of water. Simmer the mixture for 2 to 3 minutes. Serve immediately on a shallow plate.

Note: I like to use hoisin sauce for this, but you can use black bean or oyster sauce if you prefer.

Orecchiette Con L'astice
Chef Rob Gentile (Buca)

Orrecchiette has always been one of my favorite pastas to make by hand. During the summertime at Buca, we make a couple of thousand a day for this dish. Once you learn the technique, handmaking a few hundred of these little ears is quite simple. Lobster is a great addition. I prefer to use Nova Scotia lobster. In this recipe, the sweet lobster meat is complemented with garden fresh tomatoes, zucchini flowers, and summer lavender.

SERVES 4

Pasta
800 g semolina
10 g kosher salt
360 ml water

Lobster
2 lemons, halved
1 onion, diced
1 Tbsp black peppercorns
Kosher salt
2 lobsters (approximately
   4 lb total)

Lobster Butter
¼ lb butter
Lobster roe (from both lobsters)

Pasta Sauce
¼ cup extra virgin olive oil
¼ cup finely chopped onion
1 baby zucchini, skin on,
   sliced into 12 thick pieces
20 cherry tomatoes, halved
1 Tbsp crushed pink
   peppercorns
1 cup white wine
22 pieces zucchini blossom
15 leaves young basil
15 leaves candy cane mint
4 sprigs fresh lavender

1. To make the pasta, place the semolina and salt in the bowl of a stand mixer with the water. Using the dough hook, mix on low speed for 2 to 3 minutes, or until fully incorporated. **2.** Place the pasta dough on a clean work surface and knead by hand for about 1 minute, or until the dough is very smooth. Wrap in plastic wrap and refrigerate for 4 to 6 hours to allow the dough to relax before you roll it out. **3.** Line a baking sheet with parchment paper. **4.** Cut the dough into four equal pieces. Roll each quarter out by hand into ½-inch diameter logs. Working with one log at a time, cut the dough into ½-inch pieces. Place the pieces cut side up, evenly spaced, on a wooden cutting board. Using a butter spreader, flatten each piece, scraping toward you while applying pressure. The dough should curl up under the spreader like a little ear (*orecchiette* means "little ears"). Pick up each curled piece and turn it inside out over your thumb to form a shell shape. Place each piece on the baking sheet and allow to dry for approximately 4 to 6 hours. The dough can be made up to 1 week in advance, and the pasta can be stored for up to 2 days once it's dry. **5.** For the lobster, place the lemon halves, onion, and peppercorns in a large stockpot. Season with salt and bring to a boil. Add both lobsters and cook for 7 minutes. **6.** While the lobsters are cooking, prepare an ice bath in a vessel big enough to submerge the lobsters completely. The bath should be composed of equal parts cold water and ice. **7.** After 7 minutes of cooking, remove the lobsters and shock them in the ice bath to stop the cooking process. They will not be fully cooked at this stage. Once the lobsters have cooled enough to handle, remove the meat. Reserve the roe for the lobster butter. Cut the lobster meat into 1-inch pieces and set aside. **8.** For the lobster butter, bring the butter to room temperature and place it in a mixing bowl. Using a paddle attachment, whip the butter on high speed for 3 minutes. Slow the mixer down to its lowest speed and add the lobster roe. Return to high speed and mix until the roe is nicely incorporated. **9.** Line a small, shallow food container with plastic wrap and spread the butter evenly across the bottom. Refrigerate until it is cold and hard. When you are ready to make the sauce, remove the lobster butter from the container, peel off the plastic wrap, and cut the butter into 1-inch cubes. **10.** Bring a large pot of

water to a boil and season generously with salt. The water should taste like seawater. **11.** Meanwhile, prepare the sauce. Warm the oil in a medium-sized frying pan over medium-high heat and sweat the onion for approximately 5 minutes or until translucent. Add the zucchini slices, cherry tomato halves, and crushed peppercorns. Sauté for 2 minutes, until the tomatoes have started to soften. Deglaze the pan with the white wine, then add 16 zucchini blossoms, 9 basil leaves, the mint, and the lavender. Sauté for another 2 to 3 minutes, then set aside. **12.** Drop the pasta into the boiling water and cook for 4 to 6 minutes, until al dente. Drain, reserving 1 cup of the cooking water. **13.** Return the frying pan with the vegetables to medium-high heat. Add the cooked pasta and lobster meat. Season with salt and pepper and add ¼ cup of the reserved pasta cooking water to help create a sauce, gradually adding more if needed for desired consistency. When the mixture is hot, remove the frying pan from the heat and start to add the lobster butter, one cube at a time, until melted and creamy. **14.** Divide the pasta between four bowls and garnish with the reserved basil leaves and zucchini blossoms.

Note: You'll see that I've used grams and milliliters to measure the pasta ingredients. These are more accurate measurements and accuracy is key for high-quality pasta.

SERVES 2 TO 4

Fettuccine

2 ½ cups flour

4 eggs

¼ tsp kosher salt

2 Tbsp extra virgin olive oil

Sauce

1 live lobster (about 1 ¼ lb), boiled and meat removed (see pages 17–23)

1 Tbsp salted butter

6 white onions, finely chopped

1 clove garlic, minced

½ cup heavy cream

1 ½ oz spiced rum

4 sprigs fresh tarragon, finely chopped

Kosher salt and freshly ground pepper

Zest of 1 lemon

FETTUCCINE WITH LOBSTER AND TARRAGON RUM CREAM SAUCE

If you're feeling adventurous and you want to push your culinary self, give this great recipe a try. Just remember these few simple tips when making pasta from scratch:

1. Use a pasta machine when possible.
2. Have two or three clean towels handy for covering the pasta while it's drying.
3. Always have your rolling pin ready to use.

1. For the fettuccine, pour 2 cups of the flour into a mound on a clean, flat work surface. Using your fingers, make a well in the middle of the flour and add the eggs. Using a fork, beat the eggs and begin to move the flour inward, starting with the inner rim of the flour-well wall. Beat the flour and eggs together to create a dough. **2.** Using the palms of your hands, knead the dough. Add the remaining ½ cup of the flour very gradually if the dough is too sticky. Once the dough is in a ball shape, continue to knead for another 3 minutes, remembering to dust your board with flour when necessary. Divide the dough into two, wrap each half in plastic wrap, and set aside for 30 minutes at room temperature. **3.** Using a rolling pin or pasta machine, roll out each half of the dough so that it is about ¼ inch thick (it will be 8 to 10 inches long and about 4 inches wide). Using a knife or pizza cutter, slice the pasta into strips ¼ inch wide and dust them with flour. **4.** Fill a large stockpot with water and add the Kosher salt. Add the olive oil and bring to a boil over high heat. Add the pasta and cook for 5 to 6 minutes, or until it floats. Cook until firm but not hard. The pasta should be al dente. Drain the pasta and place it in a bowl until needed. **5.** For the sauce, finely chop the lobster meat and place it in a bowl. Set aside. **6.** In a large saucepan, melt the butter, then add the onions and garlic, and cook for 3 minutes over medium heat or until the onion is translucent. Add the cream and rum, turn down the heat to low, and simmer, uncovered, for 5 minutes, or until the sauce starts to thicken. Add the lobster meat and tarragon. Season to taste with salt and pepper. Mix well. **7.** Add the cooked fettuccine and mix well to ensure that the pasta and lobster are completely covered in the cream sauce. **8.** Garnish with lemon zest to serve.

Note: You can substitute cognac for the spiced rum if you prefer. I like to use spiced rum for an added kick. My favorite is Sailor Jerry Rum.

LOBSTER RAVIOLI IN BROWN BUTTER SAUCE

What's your favorite pasta? Mine has to be ravioli, especially this one. It's a great fall and winter recipe that will warm your belly and your heart.

SERVES 2 TO 4

2 ½ cups flour
1 cup hot water
1 live lobster (about 1 ¼ lb),
    boiled and meat removed
    (see pages 17–23)
1 clove garlic, minced
2 Tbsp finely chopped
    fresh tarragon
Kosher salt and freshly
    ground pepper
2 Tbsp extra virgin olive oil
4 eggs, beaten
½ cup salted butter
¼ cup crushed pine nuts
Zest of 1 lemon

1. In a large bowl, stir the flour and water with a wooden spoon until combined into a ball shape. Cover with plastic wrap or a damp cloth and let sit for 1 hour at room temperature. **2.** Finely chop the lobster meat and place it in the bowl of a food processor. Add the garlic, tarragon, and salt and pepper to taste. As you pulse the mixture, drizzle in the olive oil. Keep pulsing until the mixture is smooth. **3.** Divide the dough into two pieces and press each one as flat as you can with your hand. **4.** Lightly flour a work surface and, using a rolling pin or pasta machine, roll out one piece of dough to about ½ inch thick. As you do this, keep the other piece covered in plastic wrap until you are ready to roll it out as well. **5.** To make the ravioli, use a 2-inch cookie cutter to cut the dough into circles (or use a knife to cut it into 2-inch squares) and place a spoonful of filling in the center of each piece. Brush the edges with the beaten egg, then cover with another piece of dough to seal. Place the ravioli on a baking sheet dusted with flour and refrigerate, uncovered, for 30 minutes to 1 hour. **6.** Over high heat, bring a large saucepan of salted water to a boil and cook the fresh ravioli for 2 to 3 minutes. Drain and set aside. **7.** To prepare the brown butter sauce, melt the butter in a frying pan over medium-high heat, whisking constantly, for about 2 minutes, until the butter starts to boil. Continue to melt for a further 1 minute or until it browns. Remove from the heat immediately and whisk again. **8.** To serve, place the ravioli on a dish, spoon brown butter sauce overtop, sprinkle with crushed pine nuts, and finish with freshly grated lemon zest. Serve immediately.

Note: You can also grate some of your favorite hard cheese over the finished dish.

LOBSTER MAC 'N' CHEESE

My cooking style is fun and simple, with a focus on comfort foods. Who doesn't like to eat food that puts them in a good state of mind and belly? Canada seems to be cold for nine months of the year, and a quick dish like this one always comes in handy when you want to stay warm. In my opinion, mac 'n' cheese *has* to be made with old-school macaroni noodles like momma used to use.

SERVES 4

1 live lobster (about 1 ¼ lb), boiled and meat removed (see pages 17–23)
2 Tbsp salted butter
2 Tbsp flour
2 cups milk
1 Tbsp ground nutmeg
1 tsp Old Bay Seasoning (or your favorite seafood seasoning)
Kosher salt and freshly ground pepper
2 cups shredded aged white Cheddar cheese
3 cups elbow macaroni noodles
¾ cup panko breadcrumbs

1. Finely chop the lobster meat and place it in a bowl. Set aside. **2.** Preheat the oven to 375°F. **3.** In a saucepan, melt the butter over medium heat. Add the flour and cook, stirring, for 1 minute. Whisk in the milk until the mixture is smooth. Bring to a simmer, continuing to whisk until it has thickened. Sprinkle with the nutmeg, seafood seasoning, and a pinch of salt and pepper. Stir in 1 cup of the cheese until it has melted and the sauce is smooth. **4.** In a large saucepan of boiling salted water, cook the pasta for 6 to 7 minutes, or until it is al dente. Drain and return to the saucepan. Stir in the cheese mixture and add the lobster meat. Mix thoroughly. **5.** Transfer the pasta and sauce to an 8- x 12-inch baking dish. Top with the breadcrumbs and remaining 1 cup of of the cheese. Bake for 15 minutes, or until the cheese is bubbly and brown. Serve immediately.

`Note:` For different takes on this dish, substitute the aged Cheddar with blue cheese or Guinness Cheddar, or incorporate hot sauce throughout the dish for some kick.

LOBSTER LASAGNA

Comfort Italian food is the best when you're really hungry. When I was designing my first menus, this one topped my list of specials—it's a warm, friendly dish.

SERVES 6 TO 8

2 live lobsters (about 1 ¼ lb each), boiled and meat removed (see pages 17–23)
12 lasagna sheets
2 ears fresh corn
¼ cup salted butter (plus extra for greasing the baking dish)
3 heads garlic, minced
1 Tbsp flour
¾ cup heavy cream
Kosher salt and freshly ground pepper
1 cup spinach, roughly chopped
3 large carrots, diced
1 large white onion, finely diced
2 cups shredded Cheddar cheese
½ cup grated Parmigiano-Reggiano cheese
1 cup ricotta cheese
1 Tbsp capers
1 tsp Kosher salt

1. Roughly chop the lobster meat and place it in a bowl. Set aside. **2.** Cook the lasagna sheets according to the package directions. Cool then dry on a kitchen towel. **3.** Preheat the oven to 375°F. **4.** Grease a 9- x 13-inch baking dish with a little bit of butter and set aside. **5.** Using a sharp knife, scrape the kernels off both corn cobs into a bowl. Set aside. **6.** In a hot frying pan, melt the ¼ cup butter, then add the garlic and flour. Cook for 2 minutes over medium heat, or until the butter is melted and the garlic softens. Whisk in the cream until the sauce thickens. Season to taste with salt and pepper. Add the spinach, carrots, onion, and corn kernels. Stirring constantly, add ½ cup of the Cheddar cheese and the Parmigiano-Reggiano cheese and cook for 3 to 4 minutes, or until the sauce has thickened further. Do not bring to a boil. Remove from the heat and set aside. **7.** Combine the lobster meat with the ½ cup of the Cheddar cheese, the ricotta, capers, and salt. Gently mix and set aside. **8.** Pour a layer of vegetable sauce over the bottom of the prepared baking dish and then place four cooked lasagna sheets on top. Top this with half of the lobster mixture, followed by another layer of four cooked lasagna sheets. Add the remaining lobster mixture, top with the final four cooked lasagna sheets, and pour over the remaining vegetable sauce. Finish with the remaining 1 cup of the Cheddar cheese. **9.** Cover with aluminum foil and bake for 35 to 40 minutes. Remove the foil and bake, uncovered, for an additional 5 to 10 minutes, or until the cheesy top has browned. Remove from the oven and allow to cool before serving.

Rock Lobster Pizza
Chef Rocco Agostino
(Pizzeria Libretto)

SERVES 2 TO 4

2 lobster tails, steamed
(see page 22)
⅓ cup mayonnaise
2 Tbsp lemon juice
1 Tbsp Bomba or Italian chili
pepper sauce
1 Tbsp chopped chives
2 tsp celery salt
1 tsp Spanish paprika
¼ cup unsalted butter
1 ready-made pizza base
(12 to 14 inches in
diameter), store-bought
¼ cup grated mozzarella
cheese
¼ cup grated Stracciatella
cheese

This item was featured on our recipe for just one night: the evening of the grand opening of Rock Lobster on Ossington Avenue. We wanted to show our support and to welcome them to the community.

1. Chop the lobster meat into bite-sized pieces. **2.** In a bowl, mix together the lobster meat, mayonnaise, lemon juice, Bomba, chives, celery salt, and paprika. Set aside. **3.** Place the butter in a saucepan and let it brown. Do not allow to burn or turn black. Set aside. **4.** Preheat the oven to 500°F. If you have a pizza stone, preheat that as well. **5.** Scatter both cheeses evenly over the pizza base, leaving about 1 inch uncovered around the outside for the crust. Drizzle all the brown butter evenly over the cheese. Bake the pizza for about 8 minutes or until a golden crust develops. **6.** Remove the pizza from the oven and transfer to a cutting board. Scatter the lobster mixture evenly overtop. Slice the pizza and enjoy a little taste of the east coast.

Note: Bomba is an Italian condiment, and can be found at most specialty food stores.

SOUTHERN FRIED LOBSTER

You can do anything with lobster—and that includes frying it. Serve this one in a big bucket for everyone to share.

1. In a medium-sized saucepan, heat the oil to 350°F over high heat. **2.** In a large mixing bowl, combine the flour, breadcrumbs, onion powder, garlic powder, and salt and pepper to taste. Add the buttermilk and milk. Mix well and set this batter aside. **3.** Butterfly the uncooked lobster tails. Cut down the center of the back of the lobster shells with a pair of kitchen shears. Pull the meat out of the shells, leaving it attached at the end of the tail. Dredge each lobster tail and shell in the batter. **4.** Fry the lobsters in batches of two in the oil for 4 to 5 minutes, or until the meat is opaque. **5.** Serve the hot lobster tails with your favorite dip—mine is ranch.

SERVES 4

6 cups peanut or canola oil
    (for frying)
2 cups flour
2 cups panko breadcrumbs
1 Tbsp onion powder
1 tsp garlic powder
Kosher salt and freshly
    ground pepper
2 cups buttermilk
1 cup milk
4 fresh frozen lobster tails,
    thawed

HOG TOWN LOBSTER AND BACON STUFFED POTATOES

Toronto, the place I call home, is a city with a real love of bacon. One of my dear friends goes by the nickname Von Bacon because of how much he loves his swine! This dish is for you, VB!

SERVES 4

1 live lobster (about 1 ¼ lb), parboiled and meat removed (see pages 17–23)
4 baking potatoes
8 slices bacon, diced
3 green onions, finely chopped
½ cup cubed Brie cheese
¼ cup milk
Kosher salt and freshly ground pepper
1 bunch chives, chopped

1. Roughly chop the lobster meat and place it in a bowl. Set aside. **2.** Preheat the oven to 400°F. Line a plate with paper towel. **3.** Prick the potatoes all over with a fork to allow for air flow. Place directly on an oven rack and bake for 40 to 45 minutes, or until soft. Take the potatoes out of the oven and turn down the oven temperature to 350°F. **4.** In a medium-sized frying pan, cook the bacon pieces over medium heat until they are soft and brown. Add the green onions and cook for 1 minute to heat through. Scoop the bacon and green onions onto the prepared plate to absorb any excess oil. **5.** Slice the tops off each potato. Using a spoon, scoop out the inside of each potato. Place the hollowed-out skins in a baking dish. **6.** In a mixing bowl, combine the lobster, potato flesh, cheese, bacon, green onions, and milk. Mix until almost smooth. Season to taste with salt and pepper. Spoon the mixture into the potato skins, place them directly on a baking sheet, and bake for 12 to 15 minutes, or until the filling is heated through and the cheese has melted and is golden on top. **7.** Serve the potatoes immediately, garnished with chopped chives.

Note: I like to use Brie but you can use whatever cheese you prefer.

LOBSTER POT PIE

My love affair with pot pies started back in 2000 when I was working in a great little pub in Edinburgh, Scotland, and living above it with my sister, Amie. Each day, we made different pot pies, with fillings ranging from steak and kidney, to wild mushroom, to prawns. Here is my recipe with—you guessed it—lobster!

SERVES 4

Pie Crust

2 cups flour
1 tsp kosher salt
1 cup salted butter, chilled
½ cup warm water
2 large eggs, beaten

Filling

1 live lobster (about 1 ¼ lb), boiled and meat removed (see pages 17–23)
¼ cup salted butter
1 medium white onion, diced
1 bulb fennel, diced
1 cup fish stock
1 cup frozen peas, thawed
½ cup minced fresh flat-leaf parsley
3 Tbsp heavy cream
Kosher salt and freshly ground pepper

1. For the pie crust, combine the flour and salt in a bowl. Cut in the chilled butter to give the mixture a coarse crumb texture. Add the water, 1 Tbsp at a time, mixing it in gently with a fork. Try not to overwork the dough or it will become tough. **2.** Split the dough into two pieces. Roll each piece into a ball, then flatten it slightly using the palm of your hand. Transfer to a baking sheet, cover, and refrigerate for at least 30 minutes. **3.** Generously dust a work surface with flour and, using a rolling pin, roll out the dough to no more than ¼ inch thick. Use a 3-inch pastry or cookie cutter to cut out four circles of dough for the pie crust tops and set aside at room temperature until needed. **4.** For the filling, cut the lobster meat into small bite-sized cubes and place it in a bowl. Set aside. **5.** Preheat the oven to 375°F. **6.** In a large saucepan, melt the butter over medium heat. Add the onion and fennel and cook for 3 to 5 minutes, or until the onion is translucent. Add the fish stock and bring to a simmer. Once simmering, turn down the heat to low, cooking for 3 to 5 more minutes. Remove the saucepan from the heat and stir in the lobster meat, peas, parsley, and cream, and season to taste with salt and pepper. Allow to cool. **7.** Divide the pot pie filling between four 3-inch ramekins. Place a circle of pastry on top and seal the lid of the ramekin. **8.** Cut three small slits in the top of each pie crust to allow the steam to escape. Brush the pie tops with the beaten egg and bake for 35 minutes, or until the crust is golden brown. Allow to cool slightly before serving.

Note: You will need four 3-inch ramekins for this recipe.

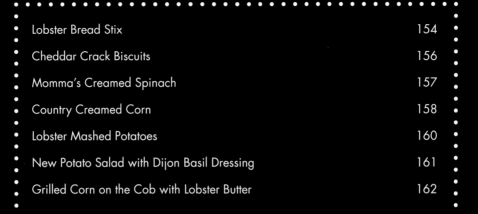

SIDES

LOBSTER BREAD STIX

Warm lobster breadsticks are even more delicious than they sound. Dip this in my delicious Samuel Adams Lager Lobstah Chowdah (page 82) and you'll be a happy camper.

SERVES 4

1 live lobster (about 1 ¼ lb), boiled and meat removed (see pages 17–23)
Vegetable oil
3 cups flour
2 tsp baking powder
1 tsp granulated sugar
1 ½ tsp kosher salt
1 tsp garlic powder
1 cup milk
¼ cup unsalted butter, melted
Pinch of Malden's salt (or your favourite finishing salt)

1. Finely chop the lobster meat and place it in a bowl. Set aside. **2.** Preheat the oven to 450°F. Lightly grease a baking sheet with vegetable oil. **3.** In a medium-sized bowl, combine the flour, baking powder, and sugar with the salt and garlic powder. Mix in the lobster meat and gradually add the milk to form a soft dough. **4.** On a floured surface, form the dough into a ball, kneading gently three or four times. With a rolling pin, roll the dough into a large rectangle, about ½ inch thick. Cut the rectangle into 12 evenly sized sticks. Flour your hands and roll each stick into a tube shape. **5.** Place the dough on the prepared baking sheet. Bake for 12 to 15 minutes, or until golden brown. **6.** Brush the bread sticks with the melted butter after they come out of the oven and sprinkle with finishing salt.

CHEDDAR CRACK BISCUITS

These warm biscuits remind me of my childhood. And the recipe is so simple. Trust me, you have to try this one!

MAKES 12 TO 16

1 live lobster (about 1 ¼ lb), boiled and meat removed (see pages 17–23)
5 cups store-bought biscuit mix
3 cups flour
1 Tbsp onion powder
Coarse salt
2 ½ cups milk
2 cups shredded smoked aged Cheddar cheese
1 Tbsp salted butter, melted
Pinch of Malden's salt (or your favorite finishing salt)

1. Finely chop the lobster meat and place it in a bowl. Set aside. **2.** In a large mixing bowl, combine the biscuit mix, flour, onion powder, and a pinch of salt. Slowly stir in the milk, then fold in the lobster meat and cheese. **3.** Preheat the oven to 350°F. Line a baking sheet with parchment paper. **4.** Dust a flat surface with flour and roll out the dough to about ½ inch thick. **5.** Using a 2-inch circular cookie cutter, cut out the biscuit shapes, and transfer them to the prepared baking sheet. You should get 12 to 16 biscuits from this amount of dough. **6.** Bake the biscuits in the oven for 10 to 12 minutes, or until golden brown. **7.** Remove the biscuits from the oven, brush them with the melted butter while hot and sprinkle with finishing salt.

MOMMA'S CREAMED SPINACH

I have fond memories of my mom, who has European roots, making this simple spinach dish. I believe she got the recipe from my grandmother, who, to be honest, isn't the best cook, but she sure loves to make sure we always leave full after visiting. I like the sharpness that Parmesan cheese adds but you can use Cheddar or any other kind of semi-hard or hard cheese. I would pair this dish with any perfectly cooked lobster! Get the hot butter out and start cracking.

SERVES 4

¼ cup unsalted butter
1 white onion, finely chopped
2 cloves garlic, minced
6 cups fresh spinach
2 cups heavy cream
¼ cup grated Parmigiano-
   Reggiano cheese
½ tsp freshly grated nutmeg
Kosher salt and freshly
   ground pepper

1. In a large saucepan, melt the butter over medium heat. Add the onion and garlic and sauté for 2 to 3 minutes, or until the onion is translucent and soft.
2. Wash the spinach, then add it to the onion-garlic mixture. Simmer, uncovered, until the liquid has evaporated from the spinach. Add the cream and reduce again for 15 to 20 minutes. Add the cheese and nutmeg to the saucepan and stir over low heat for 1 to 2 minutes, or until heated through. Season to taste with salt and pepper. Serve immediately.

COUNTRY CREAMED CORN

Pair this classic dish with any perfectly cooked lobster. Enough said!

SERVES 4

6 ears fresh corn
¼ cup salted butter
1 white onion, finely diced
1 tsp brown sugar
¼ cup milk
2 Tbsp flour
1 tsp freshly grated nutmeg
Kosher salt and freshly
    ground pepper

1. Using a sharp knife, scrape the kernels off each corn cob into a saucepan. Add any of the corn juice that comes from the kernels. **2.** Add the butter, onion, and brown sugar to the saucepan. Cook over medium heat for about 3 minutes, or until the onion is translucent. **3.** In a bowl, whisk together the milk and flour. Add this to the saucepan. Cook for 5 minutes over medium heat, stirring constantly, until the mixture has thickened and the corn is cooked and soft. Do not let the mixture come to a boil. Add the nutmeg and stir well. Season to taste with salt and pepper. **4.** Remove the creamed corn from the heat and allow to rest for 2 minutes before serving. Garnish with a pinch of nutmeg.

GRILLED CORN ON THE COB WITH LOBSTER BUTTER

This is a simple recipe for the summer and a great way to use leftover or reserved lobster meat and shells from past recipes. I hope you enjoy it as much as I do! Pair this dish with some cold beers and a nice big Ze Lobster BLT (page 35) for a dream lunch.

SERVES 4

¼ cup frozen Lobster Butter
   (page 190)
4 ears fresh corn
Canola or vegetable oil
Sea salt

1. Prepare the Lobster Butter. **2.** Gently peel the corn husks back to within 2 inches of the base. Remove the silk and smooth the husks back into place, completely covering the kernels. **3.** Fill a sink with ice water and soak the corn for 30 minutes. **4.** Oil the grate of the grill and preheat the grill to medium, around 325°F. **5.** Grill the corn cobs, turning occasionally, for 12 to 15 minutes. **6.** Place the frozen Lobster Butter in a saucepan on the grill to melt. **7.** When the corn is ready, peel open each husk, brush with the melted butter, and season to taste with sea salt. Serve immediately.

DESSERTS

PEANUT BUTTER ICE CREAM SANDWICHES

This is a simple and fun recipe I can remember my family making when I was a kid. If you have little ones, let them help by making the crisscross markings. They will have a blast!

SERVES 4

1 Tbsp salted butter
2 cups smooth peanut butter
2 cups granulated sugar
2 eggs
1 tsp vanilla extract
2 tsp baking soda
Kosher salt
Vanilla ice cream (homemade or store-bought)

1. Preheat the oven to 350°F. Grease a baking sheet with the butter. **2.** In a large mixing bowl, stir together the peanut butter and sugar with a wooden spoon until very smooth, or use a stand mixer if you have one. Add the eggs, vanilla extract, baking soda, and a pinch of salt. Mix well to combine. **3.** Using your hands, form the mixture into eight small balls. Place the balls on the prepared baking sheet and, using your hands, flatten each one to about ¼ inch thick. Using a fork, make crisscross marks on the top of each. **4.** Bake for 8 to 10 minutes, or until golden brown. Allow the cookies to cool completely before assembling. **5.** On a serving plate, lay down one cookie as a bottom layer, spoon a big heap of ice cream on top, and cover it with another peanut butter cookie. Repeat with the remaining cookies and enjoy!

Note: For some added crunch, roll the vanilla ice cream sandwich in crushed peanuts.

ROCK LOBSTER WHALE TAIL WITH CINNAMON SUGAR

This was the very first dessert I made at our Ossington Rock Lobster restaurant location. It is still our top-selling dessert. Feel free to add your favorite candy topping.

SERVES 6

2 cups flour
2 tsp baking powder
1 Tbsp salt
2 Tbsp cold unsalted butter, cut into cubes
¾ cup warm water
1 cup granulated sugar
1 Tbsp ground cinnamon
1 ½ cups canola oil

1. In a mixing bowl, use your hands to combine the flour, baking powder, and salt with the butter and form a dry, clumpy mixture. Slowly pour in the warm water and gently mix to form a dough. **2.** Dust a little bit of flour on a clean work surface and transfer the dough to it. Using your hands, knead the dough, adding a little more flour as needed. Keep kneading it into a large ball shape, then place it in a bowl and cover with a cloth. Let the dough sit at room temperature for 1 hour to rise. **3.** Break the dough into six equal-sized balls and roll each of them out flat with a rolling pin to about 3 inches wide x 6 inches long. Place them on baking sheet and put them in the refrigerator, covered, until needed. **4.** In a medium-sized bowl, mix together the sugar and the cinnamon. Set aside. **5.** Heat 2 inches of canola oil to 350°F in a large, deep saucepan over high heat. **6.** Place one of the dough pieces in the hot oil and cook each side for 1 minute, or until golden brown and crispy. Using tongs, remove the whale tail from the oil, allowing the excess oil to drip back into the pan. **7.** Sprinkle with the sugar-cinnamon mixture while still hot and serve immediately.

Note: You can top your Whale Tail with Crème Anglaise, which can be purchased from a specialty food store, or good-quality melted vanilla ice cream. Yum!

DRINKS

ROCK LOBSTER'S FAMOUS CAESAR

In cottage country, Caesars are a way of life. Being a huge fan and new restaurateur, I knew I had to create a showstopper—and what better way to do this than by topping this cocktail off with a fresh Nova Scotia lobster tail?

1. Using a large knife, cut the cooked lobster tail in half to split it. Do not cut all the way through the shell. **2.** Rim an 18-ounce beer mug with a lemon wedge, then with steak spice. Fill the mug with ice. **3.** Add the hot sauce, Worcestershire sauce, vodka, and Mott's Clamato. **4.** Add the celery stalk and top with the split lobster tail. Garnish with lemon and lime wedges.

Note: Feel free to add fresh grated horse-radish for some extra kick. Remember to give the Mott's Clamato a good shake before you add it to the other ingredients.

MAKES 1

1 fresh frozen lobster tail, boiled (see page 21)
1 lemon wedge, plus 1 for garnish
Steak spice
1 cup ice cubes
3 dashes of hot sauce
3 dashes of Worcestershire Sauce
1 ½ oz vodka
6 oz Mott's Clamato
1 large stalk celery
1 lime wedge

BREAKFAST OF CHAMPIONS

Now, I don't recommend drinking first thing in the morning unless you're on vacation. If you are, here is your new go-to recipe!

1. Pack a rock glass with ice cubes. **2.** Pour the milk, vodka, orange liqueur, and chocolate bitters over the ice, then stir. **3.** Stick 1 cherry on a small skewer, then thread the Froot Loops on. Finish with the remaining cherry. **4.** Place the dressed skewer across the top of the glass and serve.

MAKES 1

Ice cubes
4 oz milk
1 ½ oz Froot Loop–infused vodka
½ oz orange liqueur
3 dashes of Aztec chocolate bitters
2 small Guinettes cherries
5 Froot Loop cereal pieces

Note: To make your own Froot Loop—infused vodka, place 1 cup of Froot Loops cereal in a large container. Add a bottle of vodka, reserving the empty bottle. Seal the container and place in the refrigerator for 2 to 3 days. Using a fine mesh sieve, strain the vodka to remove the Froot Loops and pour back into the original vodka bottle. Will keep in the refrigerator for up to 2 months.

WHITE RABBIT

The Rock Lobster restaurant locations are all about seafood, booze, and good times. This drink is our version of a seafood margarita. Tequila, horseradish, and smokiness make for a killer cocktail! This drink was created by my friend Josh Lindley. His passion for and dedication to his craft are second to none. Josh told me that the name of his drink is a reference to sitting around a campfire and trying to get the smoke to blow in another direction by saying "white rabbits." It took me a second to get it, but when you taste the smokiness of this drink you get the connection! You need to prep the horseradish shrub a couple of days before you want to make this drink.

MAKES 1

½ oz Horseradish Shrub
  (see sidebar)
Dash of scotch
1 ½ oz premium tequila
Juice of ½ lemon
Dash of Angostura
  orange bitters

1. Prepare the Horseradish Shrub. **2.** Place the scotch in a rock glass. **3.** Place the tequila, lemon juice, orange bitters, and Horseradish Shrub in a cocktail shaker. Fill the shaker with ice and shake well, 15 to 20 times. **4.** Double-strain the shaker's content into the glass. Add a little bit of ice for good measure.

Note: This is a staple drink in our restaurants and we serve it made with premium Tequila Tromba.

HORSERADISH SHRUB

4 cups white wine vinegar
1 cup roughly chopped fresh horseradish
1 ½ cups granulated sugar

1. Bring the vinegar and horseradish to a boil in a small saucepan. Turn off the heat, add the sugar, and stir until the sugar has dissolved.
2. Empty the contents into a jar with an airtight lid. Cover and refrigerate for 2 to 5 days. Strain off the horseradish before using. The shrub (think of it like a batch of homemade bitters) can be refrigerated in an airtight container for up to 1 month.

Makes about 3 cups

SCREW'D, BLUE'D, AND TATTOO'D

This drink is a tip of the hat to one of my dear friends, the Sailor Jerry brand ambassador for Canada, Mr. Arron Thomas. Thank you, brother!

1. Pack ice cubes into a Collins glass. **2.** Combine the rum, orange liqueur, tea syrup, lime juice, and cola and vanilla bitters in a cocktail shaker. Add ice to the shaker and shake well for 30 seconds. **3.** Strain the shaker's contents into the glass and garnish the rim with a lime pinwheel.

MAKES 1

Ice cubes
1 ½ oz spiced rum
½ oz orange liqueur
1 oz spiced tea syrup
1 oz lime juice
4 drops of cola bitters
4 drops of vanilla bitters
1 slice lime

Note: Spiced tea syrup can be found in health food stores, or specialty food or cocktail stores.

VON BACON'S RED MAPLE

This drink was created by my Food & Beverage director, Robin Wynne (otherwise known as Von Bacon), who may be the most obsessive bacon fanatic on the planet. Being from Canada, we named this drink the Red Maple ("Red" for Canada and "Maple" for the bacon-infused maple whisky). Bacon and whisky—two things Canada does extremely well!

MAKES 1

2 oz bacon-infused
     maple whisky (see Note)
2 lime wedges
Bacon rim salt (store-bought)
Ice cubes
3 oz Mott's Clamato
8 drops of Worcestershire
     sauce
4 dashes of chipotle hot sauce
4 dashes of liquid mesquite
2 strips cooked bacon

1. Prepare the bacon-infused maple whisky. **2.** Moisten the rim of a Collins glass with a lime wedge and then rim it with bacon rim salt. Pack the glass with ice cubes. **3.** Add the whisky, Mott's Clamato, Worcestershire sauce, hot sauce, and liquid mesquite. Stir with a spoon. **4.** Add the bacon strips and garnish with a lime wedge.

Note: To make your own bacon-infused maple whisky, roughly chop 12 slices of cooked maple bacon and place it in a large container. Add a bottle of whisky, reserving the empty bottle. Seal the container and refrigerate for a minimum of 1 week. Using a fine mesh sieve, strain the whisky to remove the bacon chunks and pour it back into the original bottle. Will keep in the refrigerator for up to 2 months.

SAUCES AND STAPLES

Lobster Stock

Lobster stock is expensive to buy in grocery stores, so remember to keep the shells when you cook lobster, for making your own. Add the stock to soups or chowders. I love to add it to my stir-fry (page 136)!

2 Tbsp olive oil
4 carrots, roughly chopped
2 white onions, roughly chopped
4 cloves garlic, crushed
1 head celery, roughly chopped
4 sprigs fresh thyme
2 bay leaves
1 can (2 oz) tomato paste
10 black peppercorns
1 Tbsp kosher salt
Lobster shells (from 3–4 lobsters)

1. In a 2-inch-deep frying pan, warm the olive oil over medium-high heat. Add the carrots, onions, garlic, celery, thyme, and bay leaves. Cook for 5 to 6 minutes, or until the vegetables are soft. Stir in the tomato paste and peppercorns and heat through. Remove from the heat and set aside.
2. In a medium stockpot, bring 16 cups cold water and the kosher salt to a boil over high heat. Add the vegetable mixture and lobster shells. Turn down the heat to low, cover, and simmer for 1 hour, or until the stock has reduced by half.
3. Strain the stock through a fine mesh sieve into a bowl. Discard the vegetables and lobster shells. Let the stock cool, transfer to an airtight container, and refrigerate for up to 4 days or freeze for up to 3 months.

Makes 8 cups

• • •

Matty's Seafood Sauce

This sauce is awesome for dipping just about anything. Trust me! You can add minced garlic and/or a lot more lemon juice for extra zing!

½ cup good quality ketchup
¼ cup prepared horseradish, strained
Juice of 1 lemon
4 dashes of Worcestershire sauce
Kosher salt and freshly ground pepper

1. In a small bowl, combine the ketchup, horseradish, lemon juice, and Worcestershire sauce. Season to taste with salt and pepper. Mix well.
2. Transfer the sauce to an airtight container and refrigerate for up to 1 month.

Makes 1 cup

• • •

Old-School Marie Rose Sauce

I fell in love with this sauce when I lived in Edinburgh, Scotland, back in the early 2000s. This retro, cool sauce is perfect for making a lobster or shrimp cocktail. You could even consider dipping your french fries into it!

3 Tbsp mayonnaise (homemade or store-bought)
1 tsp capers
Juice of 1 lemon
1 Tbsp ketchup
Dash of Worcestershire sauce

1. Place the mayonnaise and capers with the lemon juice, ketchup, and Worcestershire sauce in a mixing bowl. Mix well until the mixture is light pink in color.
2. Transfer the sauce to an airtight container and refrigerate for up to 3 days.

Makes ¾ cup

Two-Step Curry Sauce

Try this simple Southeast Asian staple in dishes with chicken, rice, or vegetables. Of course, I think it goes best with . . . the King of the Sea!

3 Tbsp salted butter
2 Tbsp flour
1 tsp curry power
1 cup milk
Kosher salt and freshly ground pepper

1. In a saucepan, melt the butter over medium heat. Add the flour and curry powder, whisking until smooth. Slowly whisk in the milk and bring to a boil. Season to taste with salt and pepper. Allow to simmer, whisking for 1 to 2 minutes, until the sauce has thickened.
2. Transfer the sauce to an airtight container and refrigerate for up to 1 week.

Makes 1 cup

• • •

Note: Lobster shells can be frozen for up to 3 months or refrigerated for 2 to 3 days.

RLFC Banana Pepper Hot Sauce

This recipe truly is a great match for all the fresh seafood on our raw bars. It's extremely delicious with cooked lobster tails or freshly shucked oysters. The banana pepper is a member of the chili pepper family and it has a tangy, mild taste. It ranks quite low on the Scoville heat scale, which ranks the heat level of chili peppers and spicy foods.

2 Tbsp canola oil
1 white onion, finely chopped
2 cloves garlic, finely chopped
1 banana pepper, finely chopped
1 cup white wine vinegar
2 Tbsp honey or agave syrup
1 tsp kosher salt
1 tsp freshly ground pepper

1. In a medium-sized saucepan, warm the oil over high heat. Add the onion and garlic and cook for 2 to 3 minutes, or until the onion is soft and clear. Add the banana pepper and cook for 3 to 5 minutes. Turn down the heat to low, add the vinegar and honey, and cook for 5 to 7 minutes to allow the flavors to combine.
2. Place the mixture in a blender or food processor and blend until very smooth. Add the salt and pepper and blend again.
3. Strain the mixture, removing any leftover bits of peppers, into an airtight container. Cover and refrigerate for up to 1 month.

Makes 1 cup

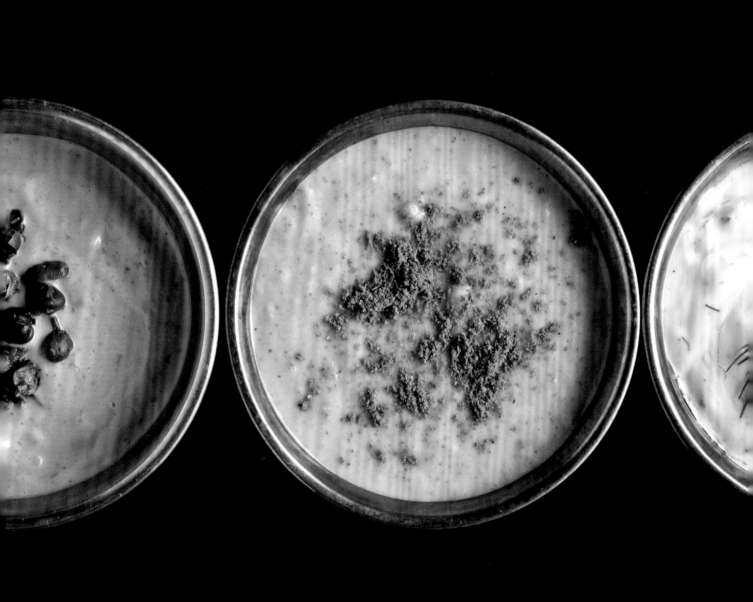

Ponzu Sauce

I love Ponzu sauce. It's a classic Japanese sauce combining soy and citrus, and it's great for dipping fresh seafood.

⅓ cup soy sauce
Juice of 2 medium lemons
1 Tbsp rice vinegar

1. Combine the soy sauce, lemon juice, and vinegar in a jar with an airtight lid. Secure the lid and shake well. Refrigerate for up to 3 days.

Makes ⅔ cup

• • •

Clarified Butter

This has a higher smoking point than regular butter as the rendered fat has been removed, making it perfect for frying seafood and vegetables. Heat this butter up and dip your lobstah for a delicious treat!

½ cup salted butter

1. In a saucepan, melt the butter over medium heat. Use a spatula to remove the bubbling froth that builds at the top of the butter. Discard the froth.
2. Pour the clarified butter into an airtight container and place in the refrigerator for up to 2 weeks.

Makes ½ cup

Lobster Butter

This is a great way to use up any leftover lobster meat.

¼ cup chopped lobster meat (you can use the meat
    from the legs of 1 cooked live lobster + the meat
    from 2 knuckles, or any other small meat pieces, see
    page 23)
½ cup salted butter

1. Put the lobster meat in a food processor fitted with a
   metal blade. Process until smooth.
2. Melt the butter in a medium-sized saucepan over medium
   heat. Add the lobster mixture and cook for 2 to 3 minutes.
3. Strain the lobster-butter mixture through a fine mesh
   sieve into a small dish. Cover the butter and freeze it
   for up to 3 months. You can also shape the butter into
   a log and wrap it in plastic wrap to make for easier
   slicing when you're ready to use it.

Makes ½ cup

• • •

Herb Butter

½ cup salted butter
1 small white onion, finely chopped
¼ cup finely chopped fresh tarragon
1 bird's eye (Thai) chili
Juice of 1 lemon

1. Melt the butter in a small saucepan over medium heat.
   Add the onion, tarragon, chili, and lemon juice. Cook
   for 3 minutes, or until the onion has softened.
2. Transfer the mixture to a food processor and blitz for
   30 seconds, or until smooth. Transfer the butter to a
   bowl and refrigerate if you're planning to use it
   that day. Otherwise, store it in the freezer for up to
   3 months. You can shape the butter into a log and
   wrap it in plastic wrap to make for easier slicing when
   you're ready to use it.

Makes about ½ cup

Lobster Cream Cheese

1 fresh frozen lobster tail, boiled and meat removed
    (see pages 21–23)
½ cup cream cheese
2 green onions, finely chopped
1 tsp Sriracha sauce
Kosher salt and freshly ground pepper

1. Finely chop the lobster tail meat and place it in the
   bowl of a food processor. Add the cream cheese,
   green onions, and Sriracha sauce. Blend until smooth.
   Season to taste with salt and pepper.
2. Scoop the lobster cream cheese into an airtight
   container and refrigerate for up to 3 days.

Makes about ⅔ cup

• • •

Spicy Sour Cream

½ cup sour cream
Juice of 1 lemon
1 ½ tsp chili powder
Kosher salt and freshly ground pepper

1. Combine the sour cream, lemon juice, and chili
   powder in a bowl. Season to taste with salt and
   pepper. Mix well.
2. Transfer the mixture to an airtight container and
   refrigerate for up to 3 days.

Makes about ½ cup

Sriracha Mayo

2 Tbsp Sriracha sauce
Juice of ½ lemon
2 Tbsp mayonnaise
Kosher salt and freshly ground pepper

1. In a mixing bowl, combine the Sriracha sauce with the lemon juice and mayonnaise. Season to taste with salt and pepper. Mix well.
2. Transfer the Sriracha mayo to an airtight container and refrigerate for up to 4 days.

Makes about ¼ cup

• • •

Seafood Seasoning Aioli

1 clove garlic, crushed
1 tsp Dijon mustard
1 large egg yolk
¼ cup extra virgin olive oil
¼ cup vegetable oil
Juice of 1 lemon
1 tsp Old Bay Seasoning (or your favorite seafood seasoning)
Sea salt

1. Place the garlic, mustard, and egg yolk in the bowl of a food processor. Mix until evenly combined. With the motor running, slowly add the olive oil in a thin stream, followed by the vegetable oil. Continue to process for 2 minutes. Add the lemon juice, seafood seasoning, and salt to taste. Pulse until thoroughly mixed.
2. Transfer the mixture to an airtight container and refrigerate for up to 3 days.

Makes about ½ cup

Cucumber Lime Granita

I like to use this granita as a garnish in my restaurants. It's great for adding a clean crispiness to oysters, salads, cold soups, or even cocktails.

1 large English cucumber, peeled and chopped
Juice of 2 limes

1. Put the cucumber in a blender and pulse until very smooth.
2. Using a fine mesh sieve, strain the blended cucumber into a small bowl. Add the fresh lime juice, stir, and place in the freezer, uncovered, for at least 1 hour.
3. After 1 hour, scrape the frozen granita with a fork to break up the mixture. Put it back in the freezer for another hour. Repeat this step three more times so that the final consistency is one of broken-up, fine ice crystals. Granita will keep in the freezer for up to 2 weeks.

Makes 2 cups

• • •

Mint Granita

⅓ cup mint leaves

1. In a saucepan, bring 2 cups of water to a boil. Remove from the heat.
2. Finely chop the mint and add to the water to infuse for 10 minutes.
3. Strain the infused water into a container and freeze, uncovered, for 1 hour. After 1 hour, scrape the frozen granita with a fork to break up the mixture. Put the granita back in the freezer for another hour. Repeat this step three more times so that the final consistency is one of broken-up, fine ice crystals. Granita will keep in the freezer for up to 2 weeks.

Makes 2 cups

Fresh!
SEAFOOD

Today's Catch

THANKS, TEAM!

A lot of late nights, boatloads of coffee, and many early mornings went into getting this book ready on time. What a ride!

I've been told by other chefs and/or restaurateur friends who have written books that the toughest thing would be to get all of the information from my crazy head or chicken-scratch notes and on to paper. After going through this experience, I have to say they were totally right! This exciting journey I live daily would not have been possible without some amazing people.

To my pops, Dad: thank you for always being there for me. I could not have asked for a better Bruce Springsteen concert partner, graphic designer, and sensational artist who has helped me, since day one, bring my brand to life. But, of course, most important, you are the best friend a son can have.

Momma, what can I say? Your little boy is all grown up and this book couldn't have happened without your constant love, support, and years of cooking lessons. You and I are exactly the same, both strong-willed and very passionate about our true loves. Thank you for giving me these attributes as you are the most caring person I know.

To my sister and part-time editor, Amie, thank you. You have such a great heart as you take so much joy in life in helping others. Never lose this, Sis. People see this and love this about you. You helped me learn to read and write, and after all these years

here we are. Who would have thought? You're the best big sister a little brother could have.

To the love of my life, Dana: you make me a better person daily. I couldn't do what I do today without your love and support at home. Life can definitely bring its challenges, but, babe, you're always there to steer me in the right direction or provide a different voice or point of view. I know we're on the right path to a life filled with rich and meaningful experiences. I love ya, Bagel!

Cheers to Robert McCullough, Zoe Maslow, Lindsay Paterson, and Terri Nimmo of Appetite by Random House. Robert, we met by chance. Some say "you need to be lucky to be good," but I think luck had nothing to do with it as your passion and professionalism brought us together. Thank you for taking a shot on a crazy guy who just really wanted to give the world a new look at lobster.

To my brand team, Marian Staresinic and Sean Beckingham at Branding & Buzzing: you guys are simply the best. The devil is in the details and, as they say, hard work pays off. Both these statements sum up how you run your lives and business, and how you respect your clients. Since day one, I've known we would form a great team destined for success.

To my amazing Rock Lobster staff and partners: I can't say thank you enough for holding down the fort while I was busy writing this book. You guys are my voice, my eyes, and the true face of Rock Lobster, and for that I thank you. They say it takes a village to raise a child—and it is exactly the same for a restaurant. What started as an idea on a piece of paper and one employee exploded in just over a year and a half. Keep pushing, guys. Thank you for being the best.

To my crazy friends who have helped me since day one with ideas, spreading the RLFC name, or actually standing in a park or field selling lobster rolls to 5,000 hungry customers for three days in a row with very little sleep at times. I love you guys: Matty C., DC, Wick, Spano, Hugo, MacNeil, Big T, Gee, Andres, Jamie, Jeremy, Ronan, Blair, MacInnis, Goat, Joel, and Fil—the list could go on forever. My parents had only one son, but I consider you guys all my brothers!

Caiti McLelland: thank you for working with this first-time author and really ensuring that my vision, passion, and voice made it onto these pages. You knew how important this was to me. Looking forward to working on the next book with you!

To Brilynn Ferguson, my amazing photographer. I still can't believe that you filmed and shot pretty much everything I did during the early stages of Rock Lobster. The best part is that after all this time, you are still capturing the amazing moments. Thank you!

Mr. Tom: thank you, sir, for taking a chance on a young man from a lake and not an ocean, a young man who wanted to show Canadians outside the Maritimes what top quality fresh lobster is. You provided me daily with the best that money can buy, and for that my customers and I thank you. I know you get a lot of excitement and enjoyment from knowing that others are loving quality Nova Scotia lobsters!

To my friends, the contributing chefs who shared a piece of their world with us in this book: I truly thank you for your contribution. It's a very exciting time to be in the food industry. I love seeing chefs supporting one another, and we seem to be at an all-time high in this respect. Mark, Claudio, Rocco, Rob, and Roger, you are all world-class chefs. Thank you for your guidance and support.

To my sponsors, big thanks. Since the beginning, working with you has felt easy and natural. Thank you, Samuel Adams and McClure's. Here's to great long-term partnerships.

And last but not least, thank you to the Toronto Underground Food Market (TUM) team, fellow street food vendors, and #LobsterLovers everywhere. Without you guys we definitely could not have done what we did. Man, collectively we certainly took the food world by storm, helping to shape it for future food-entrepreneurs. I can't say thank you enough. Love you guys!

Cheers!

MDP

INDEX

Dd

Nn

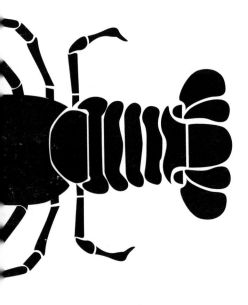

THE END